There is one truth that stands out more than any other and that is, the answers to fluid, flowing and extraordinary performance lie within each of us to be discovered when we are ready. To facilitate that journey within, Rob Polishook has written the right book at the right time to help you go inside and learn the important lessons that will transform your relationship not just with pickleball but with all of life. *Pickleball Inside the Zone* will enable you to be your best version of yourself on and off the court.

Jerry Lynch, Ph.D, Founder of wayofchampions.com,

author of 17 books including *The Competitive Buddha, wayofchampions.com*

We all know how important the mental game is to all sports! I like to think of it as the "glue" that holds your physical game, hard work and conditioning together. *Pickleball Inside the Zone* will help players of all levels effectively navigate the mental side of the game and therefore increases the chances that you'll more consistently play your best when it counts the most! . This book has an approachable, easy to understand, and proactive/interactive workbook style which will help players of all levels be their best both on and off the pickleball court."

Dr. Alan Goldberg, Mental training coach, competitivedge.com

The mental component in sport is central to consistently performing at a high level. Often, the psychological skills of an athlete are most apparent in high pressure situations. It is at these moments that calm, clarity and concentration are so important for athletes. Pickleball is no different. In his fourth book, Polishook has uncovered insights, methods, and perspectives for players of all levels. Rob uniquely weaves together on-court drills, principles, articles, and worksheets whereby players are encouraged to reflect on their experiences to facilitate best practices to enhance enjoyment and performance in competition.

Riley Nickols, PhD, Counseling and Sport Psychologist, mindbodyendurance.com

As an Executive Coach and pickleball enthusiast, I recognize essential qualities that underpin success in both leadership and sports, including self-awareness, reflection, and repeatability. Having spent significant time with Rob, whether in drilling and practice sessions or in competition, it has been a pleasure to watch him not only embody these principles but adeptly impart them under pressure. His latest book, *Pickleball Inside the Zone* is a treasure trove of insightful mental strategies and techniques aimed at propelling your pickleball game to new heights. I highly recommend this compelling read for anybody looking to advance their mindset and skillset for better pickleball play and a healthy and productive approach to play, competition, and life.

Regina Zafonte, founder Next Levels Coaching, nextlevelscoaching.com

I have been working with Rob Polishook at different points in my athletic career over the past seventeen years. He has supported my mental training from my junior tennis days to becoming a collegiate All-American tennis player to playing on the professional tour. He is an exceptional mental training coach who is able to equip his athletes with a wide range of tools and build up the confidence to use them in the heat of competition. I used his Tennis Inside the Zone book to take my game to the next level on the tennis court and now I am using his *Pickleball Inside the Zone* to help me grow as a professional pickleball player. I highly recommend utilizing any and all of Rob's mental training materials to help you grow on and off the court!

Ryann Foster, Current Professional Pickleball Player,
Former Professional Tennis Player & All-American from LSU

Rob isn't just a mental training coach; he's a living embodiment of the principles he so passionately writes about in *Pickleball Inside the Zone*. What strikes me most about Rob is his down-to-earth nature. Talking to him feels like catching up with a childhood friend. His contagious drive, enthusiasm, and energy are inspiring both on the court and translate into his book. Beyond the court, Rob's love for nature and animals, reflects his deep connection with the world around him. It's a testament to the holistic approach he brings to coaching—the mind, body, spirit, and the environment all intertwined. If you're looking for a book which instills a mindset for success and well- being, look no further, *Pickleball Inside the Zone* is the book.

Krishna Yerrmosu, Leader of advanced play @UWS Pickleball in Central park

Like a skillful surgeon, Rob Polishook systematically evaluates, diagnoses, and removes the obstacles that all players will inevitability encounter in the inner game of pickleball. Polishook creatively weaves stories, drills, best practices and anecdotes with personal experience as an interdisciplinary mental training coach to simultaneously bring out your best while also empowering you to have fun doing it. Players of all levels will benefit from *Pickleball Inside the Zone* as Robs style will guide you to towards relaxation,, reliability, and resilience both on and off the court.

Sam Priven, Director of Pickleball, Stadium Tennis, stadiumtennisnyc.com

As a coach that works with the top collegiate teams, athletes and coaches across the country, I cannot stress enough the importance of providing them with tangible skills and exercises to work on outside of sessions. That is where the work truly begins and where *Pickleball Inside the Zone* comes into play. The mental training workouts in Rob's book are the foundation to creating highly aware, adaptable, compassionate and mindful athletes and people. If approached with curiosity and an open-mind, any athlete would benefit from this book because it paves the way for anyone to achieve peak performance and find more joy on the court! Rob is an incredible human with a tremendous amount of knowledge. It has been a privilege to learn so much from his books and to this day I still implement some of the workouts in his book with my athletes. If you want to pickle, or learn to get out of a pickle, pick up this book!

Ethan Saal, Founder and CEO of bmindful: Mindfulness Training
For Athletes, bmindful.co

Rob's latest book on mental fortitude in pickleball is an absolute game-changer. As a passionate player and coach, I've found his techniques easy to implement and his engaging style both in print and in person truly delightful. *Pickleball Inside the Zone* provides the tools to empower me and fellow coaches to uplift the mental game of players of every skill level. Playing with Rob is like having a Zen teacher at your side: he lifts you up, reminds you to let go of what you cannot change, and gives you the means to focus and improve your game. His newest book is a must-read for anyone keen to elevate their mental game and is an indispensable resource for coaches!

Alexander Kidder, CEO KidderCorp, Pickleball Coach at Randall's Island Sportstime

Like millions of Americans, I love playing pickleball. Rob and I crossed paths two summers ago While in the paddle line, he told me about book *Baseball in the Zone*. Unbeknownst to him, I am a life-long baseball player and at 63, currently playing in a very competitive adult baseball league. I ordered the book and began implementing many of his mental tips into every facet of my baseball play with amazingly positive results.

Fast forward, to this summer, once again in the paddle line! He shared thoughts from his newest book *Pickleball in the Zone: 32 Mental Training Workouts for Champions*. Wow, another pure winner for the Pickleball community and it's easy to read and understand! I teach new Pickleball players at the beginner and intermediate levels and play often with an advance player group. Every mental tip Rob articulates in poignant and spot on. Most Pickleball instructors focus on the mechanics of teaching Pickleball…Rob's underlying focus is on the mental side: not overtrying, playing within yourself, and choosing repeatable shots. Rob has given me the edge as I both integrate his mental tips into lesson plans and execute them when I play for recreational enjoyment. *Pickleball in the Zone* is a must read for the recreational player looking to improve their game performance, ranking and quietly get the edge on their opponent. Well done, Rob!

John Coray, President of Mid-Coast Maine Pickleball Club, USAPA Ambassador, Certified PPR Instructor, midcoastmainepickleball.com

In my years of teaching, creating, organizing, and competing in pickleball events there is one thing that is abundantly clear to me—the mental game is of upmost importance. *Pickleball Inside the Zone* is a one of a kind book in which players of all levels can relate to. Be it the on court mental drills, principals, stories, and/worksheets, a player will connect and be able to improve their game without picking up a paddle. Rob's enthusiasm, insight, and quest to learn is constant and his passion for pickleball is infectious and relatable. I highly recommend *Pickleball Inside the Zone* and I cannot wait to see the impact this book will have on players, from amateurs to professionals alike.

Eric Ho, co-founder of NYCpickleball.com

Rob's experience as a pickleball player and mental training coach shines throughout the book. Rob's focus on training the mind first gets to the heart of our setbacks and challenges and provides a detailed roadmap to playing skillfully, not with greater pressure or strain, but with more balance and ease. His trainings encourage us to look within in a whole-hearted, kind way, to stay present and focused, to let go of what we can't control, and to trust in the process. This is much needed wisdom that will allow players of all levels to advance on the court, to enjoy the game even more, and to live as healthier, happier human beings.

Vera Ruangtragool, MA, MPH, Meditation Teacher, Founder of Truly Well (www.trulywell.org), Co-Leader of the UWS Pickleball Community in Central Park

As the owner of a pickleball venue, The Exchange Pickleball + Bar, I meet players with a range of Pickleball abilities. I see first-hand the importance of the mental game in all levels of play, and I am thrilled that there is finally a book that addresses this aspect. *Pickleball Inside the Zone* is meaningful to individuals and teams of all levels. The drills, stories, graphics, etc., are clear, concise, and empowering. After getting to know Rob on and off the court, his energy, focus, and dedication to Pickleball leaps off every page of the book. It's a must read for anyone interested in taking their game to the next level.

Renée S. Melchiode, Founder, theexchangenola.com

As a sport agent for top professional athletes and pickleball enthusiast, I have seen firsthand how important the mental game is to training, competing and post-game analysis. Polishook's book, *Pickleball Inside the Zone* address all aspects of the mental game in a fun and approachable style that players of all levels can understand and most importantly adapt and apply to their individual game. This book is a must for anyone that wants to push their limits and be their best both on and off the court.

Jay Katz, Co-founder Katz Brothers Sports, katzbrotherssports.com

Pickleball
Inside the Zone

32 Mental Training Workouts for Champions

What if <u>this book</u>
could change EVERYTHING…?

Game Changer!

By Rob Polishook, M.A., C.P.C.

Pickleball on the Brain

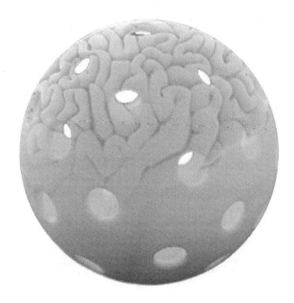

Cover Design by Kellie Patterson
Text Composition by John Reinhardt Book Design

PICKLEBALL INSIDE THE ZONE
32 Mental Training Workouts for Champions
All rights reserved.

Published and Distributed by Inside the Zone Sports Performance Group
www.insidethezone.com
rob@insidethezone.com

ISBN: 978-0-989-1862-7-8

Printed in the United States of America

PICKLEBALL is NOT your WHOLE LIFE. BUT it DOES make YOUR life WHOLE.

Contents

How to Use This Book

*P*ickleball Inside the Zone: Mental Training Workouts for Champions offers various ways to be read and experienced. To begin, I recommend browsing through the table of contents to gain a broad overview. You will notice four sections, mirroring the progression of your play: Off-Court, Pre-Game, Game, and Post-Game. Next, explore the individual workouts, each consisting of four components:

- Either mental drills, games, stories, or poems
- Principles which serve as a foundation
- A mental training article
- Interactive worksheet which ties the drills, principles, and articles together.

These four components combine to form what I have termed a "Mental Training Workout." The objective of these workouts is to provide you with experiential guidance through the mental training concepts. My hope is that they assist you in confidently and purposefully integrating the mental aspect of pickleball into your approach on the court.

Now that you're familiar with the book's layout, I suggest you read the book in one of the following ways:

You can start by selecting a random section or a specific workout that resonates with you. For instance, if you're struggling with staying calm and relaxed before a game, you can turn to the workout titled "I'm Nervous! What Do I Do? — Five Ways to Work Through Pre-Game Jitters." Once you've read the workout, take some time to reflect and ask yourself a few questions: What does this workout mean to me? How can I apply it to my situation? How can I incorporate the principles into my game? What might happen if I implement them? When and how will I put them into practice? Lastly, grab your pen and complete the mental training workout, allowing yourself ample time. Approach each workout with purpose, intention, and passion (P.I.P.). Keep in mind that each workout may take anywhere between 15 and 45 minutes to finish.

Pickleball Inside the Zone can also be experienced by reading and completing the workouts sequentially, starting from Chapter 1 and progressing through the workouts in order. While doing so, take the time to reflect on and highlight the parts that resonate with you.

Another way to explore *Pickleball Inside the Zone* is to practice the drills and games with a partner. Each one has specific directions regarding a mental intention and will help you experience the idea.

Then you can go back to the principles, article and workout. There isn't a right or wrong way to use the book.

If possible, I suggest choosing a partner and working through the workouts together. Alternatively, if you have a pickleball group, consider getting together once a week for coffee or a meal to discuss the workouts. This provides a wonderful opportunity to share ideas and insights.

Coaches, teachers, parents, and sport psychology professionals can also facilitate the workouts in a group or team setting, encouraging players to self-reflect and share their experiences. They can help by identifying the key points and discussing how pickleball players can effectively implement the teachings.

Remember, every level of pickleball presents a new set of challenges and obstacles. This is not necessarily negative; it's simply a fact! Stay patient and committed, even when things become difficult. I assure you, it won't be easy, but it will undoubtedly be worth it!

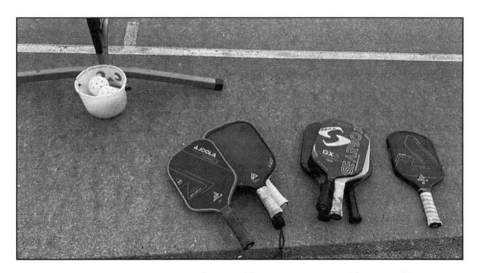

A journey of a thousand miles starts with a single (paddle) step!
—Lau Tzu.

What Are Mental Training Workouts?

*P*ickleball Inside the Zone: Mental Training Workouts for Champions allows you, whether you're a pickleball player, coach, or parent, to seamlessly integrate the mental game into the physical game of pickleball. By dedicating time and discipline to the mental game, you can significantly improve your overall performance on the court. Throughout the years, I have observed players who made time for drills during practice and focused on fitness, strength, and conditioning. The same level of commitment and intention must be applied to the mental game as well, as it serves as the "glue" that holds everything together.

Pickleball Inside the Zone consists of 32 cutting-edge mental training "workouts." Each workout focuses on a specific mental training principle, such as the importance of focusing on what you can control, utilizing imagery to prepare for each game, establishing personal routines, or effectively managing negative self-talk. Each workout includes quotes and drills, key principles, an in-depth article, and an interactive experiential workout designed for pickleball players to complete.

Improving a player's mental game is a time-consuming process. It involves experiencing moments of control, frustration, and sometimes a lack of visible progress. In fact, it is similar to learning a subtle aspect of the game,

such as executing a speed up off a dink. Developing the proper form and getting a sense of the motion takes time. Afterward, the focus shifts to controlling the paddle at impact and gaining enough confidence to execute it during competitions. Each step builds upon the previous one, akin to the growth of a tree: starting with the seeds, then the roots, followed by the trunk, branches, leaves, and finally, the fruits!

The discipline to allocate dedicated time for completing mental game workouts demonstrates dedication, understanding, and purpose. In many cases, the impact of the mental game is not even considered by pickleball players until they have a bad game or a negative experience on the court. I know this because most of my clients come seeking my mental training services during such moments. It feels as if my phone is ringing incessantly, akin to a fire alarm going off! However, the loss itself is never the problem but rather a symptom of underlying issues which are not being seen or addressed.

By reading and completing the workouts in Pickleball Inside the Zone, players, parents, and coaches can embrace a fun, systematic, and personally experiential approach to enhance their confidence in the mental game. Numerous players are unaware that it is not solely physical talent that sets high-level players apart, but rather their ability to leverage the mental game.

How Will Mental Training Workouts Help You? ... and Other FAQs

*P*ickleball Inside the Zone is intended to help you master the mental game of pickleball. It is designed to provide you with key mental strategies for specific situations you encounter throughout each game, so that you no longer struggle with distractions, loss of focus, pressure, concentration, making proper adjustments, or prolonged slumps.

Pickleball Inside the Zone will help you discover your unique strengths and make them even more potent, while identifying and moving beyond challenges, obstacles, and blocks that get in the way of your peak performance. It will help you reflect on yourself as a person and a player, honing in on the best practices for you as an individual. The book can be seen as a mirror, helping you take a step toward becoming the best version of yourself both on and off the court.

Pickleball Inside the Zone can help you improve as a player on the court and in tournaments without even swinging a paddle!

It can help you:

- adapt and adjust from shot to shot.
- execute like you do in drills during your games.
- manage pressure, tension and slow the game down.

- stay focused on the moment and let go of distracting or uncontrollable factors.
- embrace challenges, pressure, and competition.

Who should read this book?

Pickleball Inside the Zone was written for athletes of all sports, with a special focus on pickleball players. It also serves coaches, parents, and even fans, helping them understand and relate to what their pickleball player is experiencing. Additionally, it provides valuable ideas to support the individual. The book offers practical value-added stories, quotes, exercises, and worksheets to help players progress in their journey toward achieving their personal best.

Why is this book different?

Pickleball Inside the Zone is an interactive book designed to engage athletes and help them create a personal experience that guides them beyond self-imposed limits, expectations, and mental blocks. It will help the athlete become aware of what makes them unique and how to translate these attributes into their performance on the court.

Pickle & Paws

PICKLEBALL
ZONE
INSIDE THE

Section 1
OFF-COURT WORKOUTS

Off-Court Workouts

To the Child Within

There's a child inside of you who holds the key to your greatest dreams.
While she may be sometimes frightened by other people and events, she refuses to let go of those dreams.
She tugs at your leg for attention.
She whines for you to notice her.
She whispers in your ear of all that you can be.
Sometimes you'd just like her to go away with all that silliness.
No such luck. She's too persistent.
She's determined to get noticed.
She refuses to give up.
You've tried to talk some reason into her, but thankfully she won't listen.
Others have told her the "facts" and the limits on what's possible.
She's not interested in their "impossible."
She does not understand "can't."
She doesn't care if others laugh at her dreams, as long as you don't.
She wants you to consider the possibilities.
She wants to show you what she can do.
She will not quit until she's gotten your attention.
Her spirit can't be broken.
She refuses to stay down.
Her resiliency is awe inspiring.
Her enthusiasm is refreshing and boundless.
Harness that child within.
Learn to listen to her.
Let her guide you to your dreams.

—Dr. Alan Goldberg,
author of *Sports Slump Busting* and co-author of *This is Your Brain on Sports*

Workout 1
Mental Principles

- Focus on the process, not the outcome.
- It's not *when* you get there, it's *how* you get there.
- Redefine success beyond winning and losing—play proud, play hard and compete.

How Do I Get the Mental Edge?
Unlock the Mystery of the Mental Game

ON COURT DRILL
How to Get the Mental Edge

Purpose: To become more comfortable with basic shots, minimize unforced errors, collaboratively groove proper swing paths, and experiment with high-percentage and repeatable shots - one shot at a time.

Drill:
- Both players set an intention: hit 10 balls in a row without missing.
- Start from the kitchen area.
- Engage in a back-and-forth dinking exchange.

Progressions:
- Increase to 25 consecutive shots. Then increase to 50 shots and even 100 shots!
- Move 3 steps back from the kitchen. Initiate a rally and establish a new goal.
- Move back to the baseline and try to hit 10 shots in a row, then 25 shots in a row

Mental intention: The goal is to establish a consistent and repeatable shot. When faced with pressure during tight games, players want to maintain their composure, stay relaxed, and continue making shots, one after another. In pickleball, the outcome of games often depends on errors. Successful players are adept at minimizing unforced errors. As the ball crosses the net more times, the pressure to execute successive shots increases on the players, therefore practicing 10, 25, 50 and even 100 shots in a row is excellent practice. Stress the significance of maintaining high-quality shots.

How Do I Get the Mental Edge?

Ask any athlete how important the mental game is, and most would say it's between 50% and 99% of competition. In individual sports like pickleball, tennis, running, and swimming, the value always pushes the higher limits. In team sports like baseball, basketball, lacrosse and football, it also has great relevance. Remember Yogi Berra's famous and funny quote, "Half of this game is 90% mental." However, many pickleball players don't understand how important the mental game is, and ultimately, how to unlock the mystery of it. I believe that the first step is to take a step back and ask yourself some very important questions. By doing this, not only will you have a better understanding of the mental game, but you will also understand how it specifically applies to you and how to unlock it.

Who has the mental edge?

Three top pickleball players come to mind: Ben Johns, Simone Jardin and Anna Leigh Waters. Look past Ben's cat-like reflexes, Simone's amazing consistency, and Anna's impressive aggressive style and you will notice a common theme: their mental calmness and presence of mind even under high-pressure situations. These players have dominated the game for almost a decade, demonstrating their passion to compete, perseverance to learn, and ability to ride the ups and downs of the game.

Similarly, other great athletes like NFL quarterback Patrick Mahomes, NBA star Stephon Curry, and recently retired tennis legend Roger Federer come to mind. These players inspire everyone around them, never seem concerned with what they cannot control, whether it's a bad call, a raucous environment in a rival stadium, or a particularly aggressive opponent. They play in the moment, compete with purpose, persistence, and patience, while also showing respect for their opponents, the game, and themselves.

What is the mental edge?

The mental edge is the ability to consistently manage and rise above adversity, adapt to challenges, and play in the present moment. Other characteristics include patience, calmness under pressure, letting go of what they cannot control, and being okay when in challenging, uncomfortable situations. Athletes with the mental edge always seem to play within themselves and have the ability to raise their level when it's needed most.

When do you need the mental edge?

Really, all the time. It's necessary when you are drilling, playing games or reflecting on your performance after a match. Staying mentally balanced and composed under adversity is truly the mark of a champion. Most pickleball players can win when they are playing well, with momentum and their confidence. They are also fine when far out in front. However, the true champions are the ones who find a way to win when they are not playing their best or down a game or game points. Athletes with the mental edge take nothing for granted, give a full effort, and trust their process no matter the score or situation.

Where does the mental edge come from?

The mental edge lies within each of us. It starts on the inside and can be cultivated on the outside by people who inspire us, other competitors, and experiences. The key is to trust your individual process and focus on being your best while learning from mistakes, setbacks, obstacles and successes. Think of Michelangelo: when he bought a block of marble, he knew that the statue David was inside! Chip by chip, just like dink by dink, his masterpiece appeared for the world to see. In his mind, the masterpiece already lay within the block of stone, but his genius rested in figuring out how to uncover it!

Why is the mental edge important?

It's the glue that holds everything together. When you have it, everything flows. The player exhibits flexibility in all situations, accepts imperfection, manages adversity,

and never gives away free points. The ability to stay calm, centered and concentrated is what sets apart the best players. We all know that it's impossible to be perfect; however, players with the mental edge may not like imperfection, but they give themselves permission to miss and then play the next shot. Cutting themselves this slack allows them to relax, and paradoxically they miss less! A great mental approach is the most surefire way to walk into competition calmly and with an advantage.

How do I get the mental edge?

Each workout in this book is going to help improve your mental game. Each chapter includes drills, principles, articles, and self-reflective workouts that braid together like a steel cable helping you to become flexible and adaptable to situations that arise in games. Ultimately, these exercises will help make you mentally stronger. Many pickleball players don't understand that, similar to confidence and winning, the mental edge is a consequence of actions, behaviors, commitment, experience, and discipline, among other factors. Great players are highly self-aware and trust themselves, their sport, and their personal process. Just like practicing your technical skill set, commit to each workout, practice and compete with purpose, intention, passion, and a focus on what you can control.

How Do I Get the Mental Edge?

From your experience, on a scale of 1 to 10, how much do you think the mental game contributes to success in pickleball games?

Explain the reasons why you gave it this rating: _____
_____
_____

WHO do you know that you think demonstrates the mental edge? _____
_____
_____

WHAT is your understanding of the mental edge when it comes to performance? _____
_____
_____

WHEN do you think having the mental edge is important? _____
_____
_____

WHERE do you think the mental edge comes from? _____
_____
_____
_____

WHY do you think having a mental edge is important for your performance?

_____

_____

_____

HOW can you, as a pickleball player, improve your mental game? _____

_____

List three actions you could do right away to improve your mental game: _____

1. _____

2, _____

3. _____

If you did these three things, What would you expect could change in your performance? _____

_____

Describe how playing with the mental edge would look and feel like to you:

_____

_____

_____

_____

_____

Workout 2
Mental Principles

- A pickleball player is more than "just" an athlete. They are a whole human athlete. There is a person behind every swing.
- Physical talents usually are recognized first, however what completes a player are their personal talents and perennial lifelong experiences.
- Key is to bring who you are (the person) to what you do (pickleball).

Winning Within
Whole Human Athlete. Person First

Who Am I?

Pickleball is not who I am

It's what I do

It's not personal

I have nothing to prove

I don't have to be perfect

I don't have to impress

There's nothing to protect

I am not the score.

I am a Whole Human Athlete.

Heart. Energy. Spirit.

Winning Within

A pickleball player is first and foremost a human being, who also is an athlete; a whole human athlete. This idea may seem obvious, however, often we identify ourselves and others solely on what we do. Consider this: we are all born without a paddle in our hands, rather innocent infants who have just entered the world. Now, years later, when we walk onto the pickleball court, we haven't miraculously changed identities—we are still the same person.

It can be helpful to think of your development in sports and in life as a tree. A tree begins as a seed where the roots create a foundation, an anchor of sorts. The roots represent a person's values, belief system, cultural orientation, work ethic, and soul. Influential people in our lives, such as parents, coaches, friends, and extended family, play a role in shaping our roots by encouraging traits like moral values, personal confidence, and self-belief. Our experiences, including incidents and traumas, also influence and shape our perspective, contributing to our overall development.

A tree's strength lies in its roots, which serve as a foundation for its physical structure and the fruits it produces. Unfortunately, people often focus on the fruits (end results) rather than the roots (process), leading to a skewed perspective. But, just like a beautiful rose bush, a player's performance is rooted in the strength of their foundation.

The mark of a great player is their emotional resilience. Every great champion like Rafael Nadal has demonstrated the ability to manage setbacks, adversity, and challenges without becoming overwhelmed and to move forward. At any level in pickleball, it's essential to delve deeply and gain insights from each failure, experience, and success. When an athlete's roots are strong and balanced, they will be better equipped to self-reflect and manage adversity with calmness and success with humility.

Recall a time when you had a frustrating practice or tournament. Maybe the ball wasn't coming off the paddle as cleanly as usual or your shots were landing short. Is it possible that this frustration stemmed from something happening off the court in your personal life that was unrelated to pickleball? Perhaps you had a rough day at home, an argument with a friend, or anxiety about an upcoming tournament? These types of issues and unrelated stress can have a negative impact on performance.

Although we may wish to separate or "compartmentalize" personal, work and our sports lives, we understand how they can overlap and affect each other. Recognizing the intricacy of the player-person relationship will allow you to acknowledge that you are not a robot! As whole human beings, we are impacted by the events of our day-to-day lives such as stresses, experiences, and emotional and physical issues that happen on and off the court.

Think back, can you remember walking off the court after a heartbreaking loss, feeling disheartened and rattled? Perhaps it was during a game where you felt you should have won but lost your focus and repeatedly hit the ball into the net, or missed crucial serves. You could hear the spectators on the sidelines gasping as your embarrassment grew. You worry if that overhit serve or missed dink will haunt you during your next critical match. Our mind and body have a way of holding onto these memories. However, the key is to avoid fixating on these thoughts and emotions. Instead, acknowledge them and shift your focus to the present moment, staying low and balanced or taking deep breaths. This will allow the thoughts and feelings to pass like clouds across the sky.

Lastly, imagine this: you strain your back during a high stakes match, forcing you to sit out for two to four weeks. When you return, your friends inquire about your health, to which you reply valiantly, "It feels great. Never felt better." Yet, in reality, you are hesitant to exert yourself due to persistent, underlying pain. Then, you adjust your swing a bit to alleviate the pain but the adjustment period is frustrating and uncomfortable.

What's important to understand is that the body remembers memories of physical trauma, particularly injuries and surgeries. As a precautionary measure, it will attempt to shield itself from further harm by adapting. While most athletes recuperate from physical injuries, recovering from mental scars are much more difficult. A mindful pickleball player will recognize that something may be obstructing their progress and won't try to evade their feelings. Instead, they will work through them. In some cases, seeking advice from a specialist versed in somatic therapy and sports can prove beneficial.

In summary, when a pickleball player walks onto the court, they do so as a whole human athlete, with physical and personal talents, as well as lifelong experiences which include successes, struggles, experiences and traumas. Acknowledging, working through and learning from these experiences is vital to progress. It's not about suppressing personal issues, but rather accepting them and their impact. When a pickleball player embraces their true self and brings their whole self to the court, that's when growth happens. The fruits are a result of the roots.

Winning Within

What's your story? Pickleball Journey Line

Chronologically list the pivotal moments or experiences from your past that have contributed to shaping the pickleball player you are today. Consider events from all facets of your life, including pickleball and other sports, as well as non-sport-related encounters. Take note of notable achievements and failures that taught you valuable lessons, influential figures who impacted your journey, obstacles you overcame, injuries that set you back, inspirations that motivated you, and confidence boosters. Arrange these moments in chronological order, starting with the earliest one.

1. _____

2. _____

3. _____

4. _____

5. _____

6. _____

7. _____

8. _____

9. _____

10. _____

Plan your story...

Plot the 10 significant moments from the above list in chronological order along the x-axis, starting with the oldest events on the left. Rate each event's impact on the y-axis, using a scale from -5 to +5. Negative numbers (-5 to -1) represent negative impacts, while positive numbers (1 to 5) indicate positive effects. The middle line represents zero impact. Then, connect the dots to visualize the highs and lows of your journey.

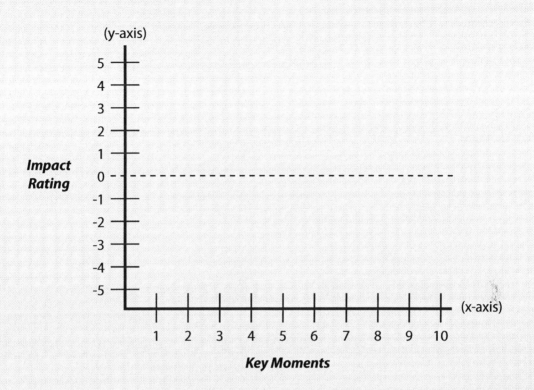

(y-axis)

Impact Rating

Key Moments

(x-axis)

As you reflect on the graph depicting the highs and lows of your journey, what does the visual make you aware of?

_____

Reflect on the instances you faced challenges or obstacles…What lessons did you take away from those experiences?

_____

Observe, what occurred after the positive or negative experiences that were not related to pickleball…What do you notice?

_____

Imagine the next five years: Describe what would you like to see?

_____

_____

Workout 3
Mental Principles

- The "Big Why" is what fuels a pickleball player.
- The "Big Why" is the intrinsic motivation that helps you persevere through challenges.
- The "Big Why" has nothing to do with outcome.

How to Get and Stay Motivated!
Uncover Your Big Why

ON COURT DRILL
Cultivating and Sustaining Motivation

Purpose: The idea is to pinpoint the primary reason you play, one that isn't centered around winning or losing, and isn't conditional upon any specific factors. Please complete the workout before doing this drill

Drill:
- Solo practice with just a ball, a wall, and yourself.
- Write down your "Big Why- why you play" on paper and keep it in your pocket.
- Hit pickleballs against the wall and focus on hitting consecutive volleys.
- If you miss or feel frustrated, remember your "Big Why." Pull it out of your pocket.

Progressions:
- Set a goal for consecutive volleys.
- As you achieve the goal, incrementally raise the number.
- Experiment with forehands, backhands, and half volleys in this drill.

Mental intention: The intention of this drill is to shift the focus away from the shots and onto your significant reason for playing (your "Big Why"). It's logical that when you're aligned with a controllable "Big Why," you're likely to engage in more practice, play, and develop a more relaxed approach. Hone your ability to recognize and connect with your "Big Why" as you rally against the wall. Practice can be fun, but only if you have a "Big Why" that has nothing to do with winning and losing. But, more so, something you can control, such as: having fun, feeling the ball, exercise, establishing a rhythm, breathing through your shots, even creating the intention to improve. Read the chapter, Big Whys are unique and personal to each player.

How to Get and Stay Motivated!

Motivation is a key factor in the success of both recreational and professional pickleball players. Exploring and nurturing motivation is a key element to every player's growth, development, and success. Lasting motivation ultimately comes from within and is rooted in a player's 'Big Why'—a personal and powerful source of inner drive that is entirely within their control. The Big Why is like a "secret weapon"; just like a secret, it is quite personal. And, just like a weapon, it's very powerful.

The "Big Why" refers to an individual player's intrinsic reason for playing, which is not related to winning, losing or the outcome. Once this reason is identified, no matter what happens on the court— whether it be a big win, a devastating loss, an injury, or a disagreement with others, (note: these are all out of a player's control)—the player can come back to their Big Why to reconnect to their true north. Making time to recognize and align with one's 'Big Why' is crucial and can enhance a player's mental game in pickleball. It helps the player stay calm, centered, and mentally balanced.

Think of the Big Why as a rudder on a boat; it keeps the boat on the proper course. Similarly, it does the same for the pickleball player. No matter what happens during a game, the player's Big Why will always remain. Big Whys can help players take the focus off of the score, a bad shot, or even an annoying opponent. After a game, they can help players get back on course if they have lost their way. Whether you're a tournament player or an everyday recreational player, living and playing according to your Big Why may require a shift in perspective. When things don't go your way, you can come back to your core reason for playing, your Big Why. Admittedly, between drilling, game play and post play activities, one's Big Why can seem stronger at certain times than others, and it can also seem a bit elusive, or even lost. However, the key is to remain true to your main reason for playing, no matter the situation.

So, what's your Big Why? Why do you play pickleball? What's your intrinsic reason for playing that has nothing to do with the outcome? It's different for everyone. For some, it's the challenge of the game; for others, it's the social aspect or the fitness benefits. Some players enjoy the problem-solving aspect of the game. For me, Rob Polishook, the author, my Big Why for playing is the challenge of the game. Specifically, the ongoing process of understanding the best way to play in different situations and with different opponents. Whether to dink or drive, to play soft or speed up—these are the challenges that keep me coming back for more. Another Big Why of mine is the synergy of playing with a partner. Together we find the best strategy, and work through obstacles, adversity, and successes. Lastly, it's the process of striving to be my best, which includes balancing drilling, recreational play, and tournaments.

It's important to take the time to reflect on your "Big Whys"—the core underlying reasons you play pickleball. To do this, it's essential to be open, truthful, and honest with yourself. Perhaps, you will find that your focus has been all about winning, trying to prove yourself to others, or showing off your skills. This approach is not sustainable because we will all come against opponents who can beat us. Even the top players in the world experience losses. On the other hand, some players started playing Pickleball because it's fun and adds a new dimension to their daily routines. But after a series of defeats, they may have lost sight of their Big Whys and become increasingly frustrated. Only by recognizing this loss of focus and rededicating themselves to the activity's fun factor, were they able to regain their motivation. Ultimately, identifying your Big Whys requires quiet reflection, but

the reward is a stronger sense of purpose and motivation.

In summary, to achieve long-term success in Pickleball, it's essential to understand that motivation is not a fleeting feeling; it's a quality that must be uncovered, developed and nurtured independent of external factors or other people. Motivation is not something that happens to you; it is something that comes from within.

Without a Big Y... you won't get the reps in! Make your shots repeatable!

How to Get and Stay Motivated!

The Big Why is an athlete's key secret to success.

When a pickleball player has an internally driven "Big Why"—a reason for playing that comes from within—they are more likely to be purposeful, be patient, and persevering. An internally driven "Big Why" is not based on winning or losing but rather on an intrinsic reason that an athlete is passionate about and has control over. This "Big Why" empowers the athlete to perform their best under pressure and in competition.

List three reasons you enjoy playing pickleball ("Big Why").

1. _____

2. _____

3. _____

4. _____

5. _____

Now, considering the above "Big Whys", rank them in order of importance to you:

1. _____

2. _____

3. _____

4. _____

5. _____

Now that you have reflected on and written down your big whys? Do any surprise you? Or do they reinforce anything regarding your purpose for playing?

_____

_____

_____

_____

_____

Being aware of your "Big Whys", how can they help to motivate you?

_____

_____

_____

_____

_____

How can your Big Why's help you navigate the ebbs and flows of the game?

_____

_____

_____

_____

_____

Workout 4
Mental Principles

- Adapting and adjusting are key components of competing.

- It's not whether you make mistakes, but how quickly you can learn from them.

- Define success based on objectives of improvement, not what the scoreboard says.

Competeology
How to be your best every time

ON COURT DRILL
Competeology

Purpose: The objective of this drill is to replicate the dynamics of an actual doubles game during singles practice, a format known as Skinny Singles. This variation of traditional singles play narrows the court width in half, emphasizing shot making, shot placement and point construction while cultivating tolerance and patience. These strategies collectively contribute to what I refer to as "competeology" – the art of competing.

Drill:
- The drill starts with the server serving the ball diagonally to the receiver's service box, mirroring doubles play.
- Only the serving player switches service boxes upon winning a point.
- As the winning server moves laterally, some serves may be directed down the line.
- If the receiver wins a point, both players maintain their positions, and the serve transfers to the opponent.
- The game concludes when a player accumulates 11 points.

Progressions:
- The game can also be played with rally scoring, attributing the point to the winner of each rally, who subsequently serves the next point.
- Games can be played to 11, 15, or 21 points.

Mental Intention: Skinny Singles is a mental challenge. Players must stay focused on being mentally resilient, playing through adversity while hitting high percentage shots under pressure. This fun practice game is truly a journey beyond the score!

Competeology

Did you know that the suffix—"ology" means 'the study of?' For instance, 'astrology' is the study of stars, and 'neurology' is the study of the nervous system. But how is this related to pickleball? Allow me to introduce you to a new field of study: 'competeology,' or the study of competition. By understanding and applying the principles of competeology, pickleball players can distinguish themselves, set themselves apart, and achieve consistent, long-term success.

So, why is competeology so important? Think of it like this: just as we need a basic knowledge of different sciences to understand the world around us, we also need an understanding of how to compete and what the process is to gain the mental edge. Competeology equips you with the tools you need to play your best and achieve your full potential.

Success in pickleball depends largely on a player's ability to make necessary adjustments during a match, whether things are going well or not. Each opponent has a unique game style, so matching up their strengths and weaknesses is key. For example, how can you neutralize a banger's shots, or a player with great hands. Furthermore, court surface, weather, and surroundings can vary from one match to the next, making adaptation even more crucial.

Competeology transforms a pickleball player into a perpetual student, constantly learning and making necessary adjustments to succeed. With the help of its eight tenets, every shot, point, game, and match become a new opportunity for growth. By mastering competeology, you can earn a practical Ph.D. in pickleball and become the best version of yourself both on and off the court.

1. Develop a growth mindset.

Carol Dweck, in her book Mindset, states that successful competitors always display a growth mindset. They see their development as a process and view mistakes and failures as opportunities for growth and learning. Competitive players analyze their errors and make adjustments to prepare themselves for future opportunities. For instance, imagine you are stepping onto the pickleball court for a challenging match. If you approach the game with a fixed mindset, you will see your skill level as static and unchangeable. As a result, when you encounter an opponent who appears to be more skilled, you will become increasingly frustrated with every mistake you make. Your errors will reinforce your belief that you are not good enough, and your frustration will cause you to lose focus. In contrast, a pickleball player with a growth mindset will approach their mistakes differently.

Instead of letting mistakes defeat or discourage them, they will develop a strategy to make the necessary adjustments. This mindset sets the stage for future successes and promotes improvement.

2. Focus on what you can control and let go of the rest.

A competitive pickleball player focuses on factors that they can control, such as effort, energy, routines, and resilience. In the game, there are elements beyond your control, such as weather, unpredictable bounces, or your opponent's performance. When a pickleball player focuses on their own game, executes their plan, and makes necessary adjustments to each point, they can walk away knowing they gave their best. By letting go of external factors and focusing on the controllable ones, you can improve your game and achieve greater success in pickleball.

3. Adapt and adjust to situations.

A competitive player understands this and is always fine-tuning their strategies each time they play. In pickleball, even the slightest modifications to your approach can make a significant impact on your performance. In pressure moments, players may get caught up solely on their results, leading to anxiety and tension. This singular focus takes them away from a vital question: What can I do now, in this moment, that I can control, and that puts me in the best position to succeed? By remaining flexible and concentrating on the factors within your power, you can stay calm and composed under pressure.

4. Learn from mistakes.

Great pickleball players understand that making mistakes is a natural part of the game. Despite their best efforts, bad shots will happen. However, rather than becoming discouraged by failure, players should embrace it as an opportunity for growth and development. In fact, failure should be expected, and even encouraged, as it provides valuable feedback and insights that can help players refine their strategies and improve their skills. The key to success is to learn from those mistakes and use them as stepping stones towards achieving greater success on the court.

5. Never, ever, ever, give up.

Competing requires resilience and determination—the ability to never give up. A competitive player embraces challenges and setbacks as opportunities to push themselves harder. Even in tournaments where they don't perform their best, a competitive player remains unfazed and strives to win through sheer grit and determination. They have a strong sense of perspective, knowing that every point in a game is a new opportunity to excel and that what happens next is the most crucial thing.

6. Get comfortable being uncomfortable.

A competitive pickleball player understands that stepping outside their comfort zone is necessary for success. By making necessary adjustments, and pushing themselves to their limits, they remain focused on the present situation. They understand that getting comfortable with being uncomfortable is a critical aspect of their growth as a player. This mindset cultivates resilience and strengthens their overall game, enabling them to reach new heights.

7. Be aware and make high-percentage choices.

In pickleball, making high-percentage choices is akin to exercising discipline on the court. A disciplined player exercises patience when dinking, avoids unnecessary risks, and instead plays with intelligence based on the situation at hand. They remain mindful of the situation and choose high-percentage shots to stay in points and maximize their chances of winning . This ability to remain aware of their options and make informed choices is often what sets successful players apart from their peers.

8. Sportsmanship.

Competitive players respect themselves, their opponent, and the game itself. They prioritize giving their all and focusing on what they can control, always striving to play with integrity, honesty and humility. They understand that the opponent is not their enemy, but rather a partner in the game, challenging them to bring their best performance to the court. Ultimately, this perspective fosters a positive and collaborative environment in which both players can push each other to reach new levels of skill and achievement.

By following the above principles of Competeology, you will put yourself in the best situation to succeed. These concepts are entirely within a pickleball player's control and consistent practice will boost confidence throughout games and tournaments. They will enable you to stay focused on the present moment, rather than worrying about past results or future outcomes. Moreover, they will help you manage adversity with poise and determination. Ultimately, embracing the principles of competeology frees you to learn and grow every time you step onto the court, allowing you to become the best possible version of yourself as a pickleball player.

Competeology

com·pete (kə m·pēt'): 1. from late Latin competere: to strive together, meet, come together, agree; from com- [together] + petere [to seek]; 2. to enter into or be in rivalry; contend; vie (in a contest, athletic meet, etc.).

Name two players who, in your opinion, compete well:

Player #1: _____   **Player #2:** _____

List the characteristics, attributes, or behaviors that make them good competitors:

Player #1: _____   **Player #2:** _____

Player #1: _____   **Player #2:** _____

Player #1: _____   **Player #2:** _____

Is there anything on this list that the player cannot control?

_____

Recognizing this, what does this mean for you?

_____

Identify the top three characteristics, attributes, or behaviors from above that, if you improved, you would see the biggest results:

1. _____

2. _____

3. _____

What would happen or be different if you improved on the above things?

_____

Workout 5
Mental Principles

- When you let go of expectations, you let go of what's out of your control.

- The more emphasis that is placed on the outcome means less time to concentrate on what's important in the moment.

- Everyone wants to win, but what's necessary is to take a step back and ask…what's important now! (w.i.n.)

All I Want To Do Is Win!
What's important now (W.I.N.)?

ON COURT DRILL
Free Throw Shooting

Purpose: The goal in this drill is to develop ease in hitting shots during in-game scenarios that are consistent from various locations on the court. Whether executing a third shot drop, a reset volley, or even an ATP, practicing the shot is essential to ensure its repeatability and reliability, especially when facing pressure.

Drill: Engage in this live ball drill with a partner.
- One player stands at the non-volley zone (kitchen line).
- The other positions themselves three feet behind the kitchen line on their side of the net.
- The kitchen player hits balls to their partner.
- The partner responds, simulating third shot drops.
- The player executing third shot drops will hit 10 shots. They will track the number of successful shots made. For example 6 out of 10, or 60%.

Progressions: Move back a few feet and repeat the drill. Then move back to the baseline.
- To enhance the challenge, the partner at the kitchen can deliver the ball with increased pace and spin. Partners can also position targets beside the kitchen player's backhand and forehand sides, aiming to hit these designated spots.
- Partners can pick any targets on the court to hit to, and with any speed, spin, or height.

Mental Intention: The key is to remain composed, balanced, and relaxed while executing shots. It is imperative that you maintain a relaxed and light grip tension. Much like free throw shooting, as your success rate improves, the pressure and difficulty of consistently executing successful drops may also increase. This drill helps players develop a "feel" for the shot, refining their ability to execute it effectively. It is advisable to hit a minimum of 10 shots from each location, focusing on gaining a "feel" for the shot and monitoring your success rate. Remember: Just as accomplished free throw shooters practice 100 free throws daily, similarly, a principle could be applied here: "100 third shot drops a day keeps the bangers at bay!" Or 100 resets a day... :)

So You Want to Win!

Pickleball players and all athletes have one common trait—they all want to win! However, what separates a great player from a good player is the ability to focus on the specific steps that they can control and let go of what they cannot. When a pickleball player's focus is consumed with the desire to only win, they lose sight of the process and, most importantly, what's important now (W.I.N.). Pickleball is unique and full of unknowns. Each opponent, court and set of conditions is completely different and no two shots are exactly the same. When our mind is focused on the outcome, there is very little opportunity to mentally prepare for what needs to happen in that specific moment during that specific shot.

Imagine this: you're beginning a match and thinking about your opponent's record, which makes you nervous since they are undefeated. Now, imagine asking yourself the simple question: what's important now? Your answer will bring you back to the present as you might reply, "focus on my game, play softly to their backhand, and don't forget my pre-serve routines.

Pickleball players can put themselves in the best situation to be successful when they remember that winning is a by-product or consequence of letting their off-court preparation, on-court training, and instincts take over. Their attention should be focused on playing in the here and now, the present moment. Each shot and point should be about what's happening at that moment, without drifting to uncontrollable factors . Some uncontrollable factors might include focusing on a previous missed shot, sulking about a previous loss, paying attention to how your opponent is acting, complaining about the weather, worrying about the expectations of others, and comparing yourself to others in a tournament.

Being present for each shot allows you to make the necessary adjustments that are needed for that specific shot. Your attention should not be divided between the past or future; it should be solely on what is happening in the present moment. What is happening at the moment is the only thing that is important. This singular focus will allow you to adapt and adjust on each shot, and the score will take care of itself.

When a pickleball player is present with each shot, only three things can happen:

- **The player finds that they are not good enough on that day to win.**
- **The player learns what skills are needed to be honed for the next tournament.**
- **The player exceeds their wildest expectations.**

So You Want to Win!

We all want to win!

However, most people don't realize that winning is often the result of specific actions. In other words, winning is a consequence. It doesn't happen on its own. Simply wanting to win is not good enough to be a great pickleball player.

It's important to ask yourself What's important now (w.i.n.) and define what specific actions are necessary at the moment to put yourself in the best possible position to win.

On each line below, list the actions or steps that are important to prepare yourself to be in the best position to compete and give yourself the best opportunity to consistently play at your highest level.

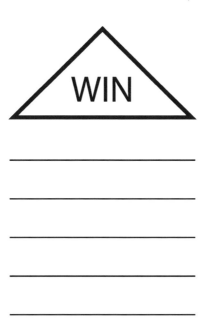

_____

_____

_____

_____

_____

Workout 6
Mental Principles

- Goals act as a compass, they can help you stay on course.

- Success is determined by how you practice your individual process goals.

- Always drill with intentions and bring those same intentions to games. Be consistent!

Goal Setting
Players don't plan to fail but, they do fail to plan

ON COURT DRILL
Around the World

Purpose: The idea of the "Around the World" drill lies in practicing accurate target practice from various court positions while incorporating movement. This drill shares similarities with the childhood basketball game "Around the World" that I used to play.

Drill:
- One player stands along the court's perimeter, delivering dinks and third shot drops.
- The other player is stationed at the kitchen, catching the shot and re-feeding either by hand or paddle to the next designated spot.
- The player executing dinks and drops shifts across different pre- designated court spots. The kitchen target remains consistent, such as the player's backhand side.
- A successful return to the target prompts another feed for the subsequent location.
- Missing a shot leads to either another attempt or the option to stay at that spot for the next turn.
- Players swap roles, sustaining the game's flow.
- The aim is to complete the circuit and return to the starting point by executing successful dinks and drops.
- The player who accomplishes an entire "Around the World" rotation first secures victory.

Progressions:
- If the ball lands in the net they can take a "chance" and try again. If they make the shot they move to the next location. If they miss, they go back to the starting point.

Mental Intention: The essential factor is to stay patient, balanced, and composed while transitioning between various court positions. Moreover, effectively handling pressure is vital, particularly as the dinking player advances. The prospect of hitting a ball short into the net, which results in returning to the starting point, magnifies the pressure.

Goal Setting

Goal setting is a great tool for aspiring pickleball players to implement during their development. Goals help the player stay committed, determined and focused. They should be challenging, individualized, and motivated by intrinsic factors that are meaningful to the player. Additionally, goals should also be specific and time-bound, so the player knows exactly what they are trying to accomplish and by when. I suggest writing down goals and keeping them in a visible place and/or sharing them with others. Doing so will help the player keep their goals at the forefront of their mind.

There are two types of goals: outcome goals and process goals. Both important but different. It's imperative to understand the distinction between the two types. Outcome goals focus solely on the end result, while process goals focus on the steps a player must take to give them the best chance to achieve their outcome goal. For example, an outcome goal might be to win a tournament, while a process goal could be to improve serving accuracy, third shot drops, or stay calm and centered between points. Outcome goals, which are result based, are out of a player's control. It should be stated up front, that we all want to win, but wanting to win (outcome goal) and doing the things that are necessary to win (process goals) are two different things. Focus needs to be on what is necessary to give yourself the best chance to win, not the end result of winning itself. This is where process goals come into play. They focus on specific areas of the game that the player can practice and can control such as how they prepare, how they drill, how they warm up, what shots they choose, what strategy they use, and how they react to situations in games.

An important aspect of goal setting is objectively determining where a player is in relation to their goals, essentially knowing "where they are." This realistic perspective will help the player understand "what they need to do" and the appropriate process goals necessary to practice to give them the best chance to achieve their goals. The most common mistake players make is focusing solely on outcome goals, such as winning. This can result in subpar, poor, and frustrated outcomes because their focus is split between what they want to happen in the future and what is actually happening in the moment, their focus is divided.

Instead of focusing on winning, which is something that cannot be controlled, a player needs to focus on playing each shot with a clear intention, in the moment, during the point. An example of this could be hitting deep returns to the middle and moving to the kitchen. Hitting shots with intention helps players maintain their focus on the process, stay fully engaged in the moment, and control what they can control.

It is recommended that players set an outcome goal and then determine the process goals that will best help them reach the outcomes. An outcome goal is like standing at the bottom of a staircase and only staring at the top step, this can be overwhelming, wondering how to get to the top. However, a process goal involves taking one step at a time. By breaking a larger goal into smaller, achievable steps, you can make progress and achieve your ultimate goal. Remember: to reach the top, you must start with the first step, followed by the next step. That's the process!

Outcome goals are static whereas process goals are flexible and can be adapted, adjusted and modified at any time.

For example, let's consider this situation of outcome and process goals: I, the author (Rob Polishook,) once lost in a tournament. Clearly, the outcome goal of winning was not met! However, upon reflection, I identified a key weakness: my inconsistency in hitting resets from the transition zone and the kitchen. Since then, I have been dedicating 20 minutes per practice to practicing reset volleys from different court locations. Think about it, this type of intentional practice is no different than a basketball player practicing their jump shots from different locations on the court.

As Dr. Alan Goldberg, a noted mental training coach, says, "Once the competition starts, the outcome goal should be parked at the gate and the player should focus on the moment and the process of what they need to accomplish." Research has confirmed that achieving process goals not only enhances performance but also reduces anxiety and builds confidence. This is because process goals are within the pickleball player's control.

Here are three examples of process-driven goals in Pickleball:

- Incorporate specific strength training or movement exercises three times per week into your workout routine to increase balance and stamina.

- Practice hitting ten serves to each of the three different targets (down the T, body, and out wide) on each side of the court three times per week.

- Practice hitting 10 reset volleys from the kitchen five times per week. Then, move back to the transition zone and repeat the process.

Goal Setting

What is a goal you want to accomplish? (outcome goal) _____

_____

_____

Why is this goal meaningful to you? (big Why) _____

_____

_____

_____

Rate, on a scale of 1–10, where you are now towards achieving this goal (10 = achieved goal). _____

_____

_____

_____

What are three specific steps you must do to achieve this goal? How often? And how long? (process goal)

1. _____

2. _____

3. _____

In attempting to reach this goal, how hard do you think it will be? _____

_____

_____

What could stop you? _____

_____

_____

Will you let it? _____

When will you start? _____

Workout 7
Mental Principles

- Change starts with Awareness. Only through self-reflection, can you get to where you want to be.

- Setbacks are a part of all players' pickleball journey. Think of setbacks like a doorway. Make the choice to step through the doorway and learn from the setback.

- Awareness and the 5 A's is a continuous cycle. What changes is your ability to continue navigating the different steps.

How can I stay focused?
Awareness and the 5 A's

ON COURT DRILL
Awareness of Out Balls

Purpose: To increase your awareness of balls that are going out! It's crucial to understand that out balls are presents from your opponents. By refraining from hitting these balls, you prevent wasting these valuable opportunities. Developing the ability to recognize and appreciate these generous offerings takes practice.

Drill:
- Have one player feed 10 balls from the baseline, each at varying heights.
- Initially, let each of the first 10 balls pass by at the kitchen line.
- Focus on the sensation of allowing a ball to go out.
- Observe whether the ball ultimately lands in or out.
- Pay attention to ball height, speed, and trajectory.
- The player feeding the balls should deliberately hit some balls out to contrast with the ones that will land in.
- Game: Play a game to 11 points, either down the line or cross-court. If the player at the kitchen wins the point, they earn one point. However, if they let a ball fly that lands out, they are awarded two points. The player at the baseline initiates the point.

Progressions:
- Instead of being at the baseline, the player can move to the transition zone and begin the point from there.
- Both players can be at the kitchen, but only permit one player to speed up.
- If the non-speeding player avoids hitting an out ball, they accumulate 2 points.

Mental intention: To help players get comfortable and aware of balls that are going out. A general guideline is to note that when a player needs to hit the ball upward, it becomes more challenging to keep it within the court. This serves as a primary indicator, especially when in proximity to the net. It's important to remember that when the ball comes high (chest high), let it fly!

What Does it Take to Win?

There is a saying, "You can't change the wind, but you can change the direction of the sails." We have all seen pickleball players on public courts, doing the same thing repeatedly, which leads to the same results. Players who refuse to make adjustments to their game, whether it's trying to drive the ball through their opponents, or not adapting to the speed of the game, always have a difficult time. Some players take overly risky shots, such as putting extra spin on the ball and missing in the net instead of hitting a more neutral shot and forcing their opponent to play another ball. As Einstein once said, "The definition of insanity is doing the same thing over and over and expecting different results."

The most important component of pickleball, and life, is the ability to be aware of a situation and adjust to it. Pickleball players need to be great problem solvers. To do this, it's imperative to have a framework in place that you can systematically apply.

This workout will focus on the framework, and what I believe to be the most essential mental characteristics for improvement, success, and ultimately reaching your personal peak performance. This framework includes Awareness and the 5 A's: Acknowledgment, Accountability, Adjustability, Adaptability, and Assessment. Without this framework, a player will be unaware of what's happening in the present moment and consequently be unable to make the proper adjustments to counter what is necessary to succeed.

Awareness: The first step in solving any problem is having awareness. Without being aware, a pickleball player is unable to assess and determine the current reality of a situation. Awareness entails simply and non-judgmentally, observing what is happening. This is especially critical as momentum and circumstances can shift dramatically on one point in pickleball. Remaining in the present allows you to accurately assess a situation, adjust, and position yourself accordingly. If you find yourself stuck on a previous shot or point, your ability to play the current point will be compromised. Similarly, if you are focused on the future, you will be unable to accurately see what is unfolding in front of you.

Accepting: By accepting a situation, you do not necessarily have to like it. If you are down by 3-9 in the decisive game, you have to accept what is happening and then decide what you can do about it and how to approach the situation. This will help ensure success! Many pickleball players often say, "Why should I accept it? That implies complacency." This is not so. Acceptance simply means that you are aware of the current reality of the situation. In effect, I am suggesting that this provides a choice and the opportunity to either make the change or do nothing.

Accountability: If a pickleball player does not take accountability, they will blame the circumstances on something else, like the weather or crowd noise, and nothing will change. This attribute can be painful but refer to this saying, "It may hurt, but the truth will set you free." It is normal to have a bad shot, game, or day. What is important now is that you take ownership of your mistakes, be accountable, and then learn and build off of them.

Adaptability: This refers to adapting internally and responding to the situation during a game that puts you in position to perform at your best. In other words, being able to mentally reframe a situation. Once a pickleball player can go from the negative to the neutral (or, preferably, the positive), they can change the situation to their advantage. Internal adaptation is imperative. Without this, nothing changes. A mentally strong pickleball player can change their mindset and turn things around. For example, recently, I was playing a match. We won the first game 11-2, played beautifully and used the soft game to set up volley winners. However, in the second game, we got behind 1-9. I point-shifted and told my partner to pretend the score was 0-0, we came back to win the next 9 points but then lost the game. My partner was down; however, I pointed out that we won the last 9 out of 11 points and our charge was to build on this. Guess what? Yes, we won the decisive third game!

Adjustability: This refers to making changes in physical or technical strategy based on the situation. Each match, each opponent, and court will be a little different. Adapting to these uncontrollable variables is the key to competing and will make a huge difference in your game. An example of this could be when your opponents have the wind behind them. Recognizing this and adjusting to high balls that will go beyond the baseline. Similarly, when you are hitting into the wind, realizing your third shot drops need a bit more loft or power to get over the net and drop down.

Assessment: This is a continual process and must be done after a player has made their adjustments and adapted. Often, a player is very close to achieving their goal, but they just need to settle in. Other times, another small tweak may be needed to succeed. Without the assessment, it is not possible to determine the results of the previous steps. Additionally, this step allows the entire process to build on itself and continue to achieve your goals.

Awareness and the 5 A's is a formula to problem solving on the court and in life. This formula can be seen being used by some of the greatest athletes ever. Think about what it takes to accomplish anything significant in life. Inevitably, awareness and the 5 A's will be necessary, whether it be taking a test, competing in any game, or winning a pickleball tournament. Remember, you can't be your best unless you can overcome adversity.

What Does it Take to Win?

ASSESSMENT
ADAPTABILITY
ADJUSTABILITY
ACCOUNTABILITY
ACKNOWLEDGMENT
AWARENESS

The solution to any problem starts with awareness!

Awareness: Name a specific Pickleball shot or situation that is troubling you. (describe it) _____

_____

Acknowledgment: What can you do to acknowledge the situation?

_____

_____

Accountability: What can you do to take accountability for the situation?

_____

_____

What Does it Take to Win?

Adjustability: What can you do to physically adjust to change the situation?

_____

_____

Adaptability: What can you do to mentally adapt to change the situation?

_____

_____

Assessment: Based on the previous steps, how would you assess things?

_____

_____

How would this process have changed the situation you just wrote about? _____

_____

_____

There is something in your heart and it's in your eyes, it's the fire, inside you.
Let it burn, you don't say good luck, you say don't give up, it's the fire inside you. Let it burn…

The Fire, John Legend and the Roots…

Workout 8
Mental Principles

- Over trying, forcing, comparing, and judging are the fastest paths to playing outside the zone.

- Trust yourself, the answers lie within.

- Remember your training—trust your instincts.

Pickleball Inside the Zone
One Shot at a Time

ON COURT DRILL
Playing Inside the Zone (5 balls)

Purpose: Let go of thoughts from the past and even future points, rather concentrate solely on the current point – in the here and now.

Drill:
- One player is positioned at the kitchen line, while the other is at the baseline executing third shot drops.
- The player at the kitchen delivers deep balls to the baseline player, allowing practice of third shot drops.
- The kitchen player can hit the ball out of the air or allow it to bounce in the kitchen.
- Points are earned whenever the baseline player successfully executes a third shot drop.
- Points accumulate over five attempts (balls) by the baseline player.
- In case the player at the kitchen makes a mistake, an additional ball is introduced, replacing the erroneous shot, this miss does not count against the player accumulating third shot drops..
- If the player hitting the third shot drop misses, their partner will feed another ball. There will be 5 separate feeds upon missed balls and players switching positions.

Progressions: Initially, shots from the player at the kitchen should be cooperative, enabling the baseline player to establish a rhythm for third shot drops. Once the player has developed a rhythm, the kitchen player can begin employing slicing and flicking volleys to enhance the difficulty of executing the third shot drop.

Mental intention: The goal is to concentrate on the ball you're currently playing. Frequently, a player might make an error with the first ball, which can influence subsequent shots. In reality, the player needs to let go of that shot and focus on the next ball.

Pickleball Inside the Zone

The "zone" is a state of playing entirely in the present moment, free from distractions that cannot be controlled, and, it exists within each of us. To play pickleball inside the zone a player must be aware, loose, and have a relaxed perspective . Playing Inside the zone requires accepting what the player is experiencing at any particular time. It is a place of not over-thinking, over-judging, over-trying or comparing. This usually results in a smooth, harmonious, effortless flow of energy that produces unencumbered play.

These moments were also defined as "peak experiences" by the humanistic psychologist Dr. Abraham Maslow. His research indicated that those who achieved such "peak experiences" felt 'more integrated', 'at one with the experience', 'relatively egoless', 'fully functioning', 'in the groove', 'free of blocks, inhibitions, cautions, fears, doubts, controls, reservations, and self-criticism', 'spontaneous and more creative', and 'in the here and now.' To sum it all up, the feat being attempted feels effortless, like flowing water.

As athletes, we are all capable of playing inside the zone. It is a natural state that is experienced rather than invented. It is not a destination that you travel to; rather it is a place that finds you when you let go of all the distractions and stay present. While not a movie about pickleball, this feeling is aptly addressed in the 2000 golf movie "The Legend of Bagger Vance," starring Will Smith as the caddie Bagger Vance and Matt Damon as the famous golfer Rudolf Junuh. Vance says to Junuh, "Inside each and every one of us is one true authentic swing...Somethin' we was born with...Somethin' that's ours and ours alone...Somethin' that can't be taught to ya or learned...Somethin' that's got to be remembered...Over time the world can rob us of that swing...It can get buried inside us under all our wouldas and couldas and shouldas...Some folk even forget what their swing was like...Close your eyes...Feel the ball..."

Pickleball inside the zone is innate in every person; in fact, each of us has already experienced this seemingly unattainable state as a young child. Upon being born into this world, the unassuming child breathes deeply and instinctively through their nose. We learn best when we are young, free from stress and outside distractions that pull us away from the present moment. Taking your first steps as a child requires trust in oneself, determination, and trial-and-error. Most children learn to walk before their parents actually teach them. They learn through observation, natural instinct, and modeling others around them. Through this process of learning to walk, one gains confidence in the natural and instinctual learning process that operates within them. Conversely, parents watch their children's efforts with love and interest, but usually without much interference. When a child loses their balance and falls, the mother does not condemn the child as clumsy or uncoordinated; she doesn't even feel bad about the tumble. She simply notices the event and provides a kind word, support, and usually a loving gesture of encouragement. Consequently, a child's progress in learning to walk is never hindered by the idea that they are not doing better. If we could only treat our adult athletic endeavors, such as in pickleball, as we do a child learning to walk, we would make tremendous progress toward uninhibited and non-comparative improvement—the stepping stone to effortless peak performance.

Michelangelo, the renowned Italian sculptor, provides a classic metaphor of focusing on the process and getting inside the zone. He sculpted the Renaissance masterpiece, David, from 1501 to 1504. Undeterred by the challenging tasks of carving a statue out of a mere slab of marble, Michelangelo had a vision of the finished product. He worked under the premise that the image of David was already in the block of stone, a concept referred to as disegno. He chipped away at the stone and brought out what others could not even imagine. He saw and knew what others did not. The marble he was chipping away at was a metaphor for the distractions, limitations, fears, anxieties, negative self-talk, and uncontrollable events that get in most people's way. Michelangelo knew David existed, but he had to let him appear. Similarly, our best performances are waiting to happen once we let go of distractions, fear of failure, and our ego.

It can be challenging to play pickleball in the present. However, by focusing on your breath, the present situation, and your routines, you can. While learning from the past and setting future goals are helpful, while playing it's imperative to let go of these thoughts and compete in the moment.

The body has the gift of being constantly centered and present. To access the part of ourselves that has the power to transform our life experiences and enable us to perform without limits, we need to bring our awareness to our body, breath, senses, and start from the inside out, like the calm eye of a hurricane amidst the unpredictable outer storm. Bagger Vance understood this truth, saying, "There's only one shot that's in perfect harmony with the field… there's a perfect shot out there tryin' to find each of us…All we got to do is get ourselves out of its way, to let it choose us…Seek it with your hands. Don't think about it…Feel it."

Pickleball Inside the Zone

Remember a time…when everything was flowing and you were playing Pickleball inside the zone.

When was it? _____

What time was it? _____

Where was it? _____

How old were you? _____

What were you wearing? _____

What was the weather? _____

Who was watching? _____

What did it feel like? _____

What smells did you notice? _____

What was happening? _____

What sounds did you notice? _____

What was your sense of time? _____

What was going through your head? _____

Overall, what words or images come to mind? _____

_____

What else do you remember about that time you were playing Inside the Zone?

_____

_____

_____

Try connecting to a time you played inside the zone and bring up the image in your mind. This will help you to let go, settle, and relax before playing your next point, practice or game.

How can you use your 'Inside the Zone' image to help you? _____

_____

_____

_____

_____

_____

_____

Workout 9
Mental Principles

- Feel It, See It, Imagine It.
- Imagine...what if there was no problem to solve?

Mental Imagery!
How It Can Help Your game

ON COURT DRILL
Imagery with Lunges

Purpose: The concept behind this drill is to enhance flexibility and strength by combining pickleball movements with visualizing the shots you would hit. This drill serves as an excellent warm-up before game play or as a valuable addition to your fitness routine.

Drill: Lunges:
- Begin with your feet together.
- Step forward with your left foot, ensuring your knee does not extend beyond a 90-degree angle.
- Allow your back leg (knee) to lightly touch the ground.
- Return the left foot to the standing position.
- Lunge forward with the right foot.
- Return to the full standing position.

Progressions:
- Perform lunges every other day.
- Complete 1 set of a larger number of lunges.
- Divide the total number of lunges into 4 sets.
- Gradually progress, add 5 lunges each week, increasing the overall count as comfort allows.
- Engage in lunges that correspond to the number of hits executed by a player or team.

Mental Intention: The key aspect is to envision that as you perform lunges, you're simultaneously executing a shot—feel free to hold a paddle in your hand. Essentially, each lunge transforms into a visualization of a shot. Consider that during an average point comprising 4-12 shots, a player should feel at ease completing an equivalent number of lunges and then repeating it for the next point. If fatigue sets in during this exercise, it's likely that fatigue would also affect game play, potentially compromising a player's ability to perform at their best due to fitness limitations.

Mental Imagery!

What images come to mind when you hear phrases such as "imagine if…" or "remember a time when…?" For most people, these words trigger flashbacks of certain situations or moments on or off the court. Can you recall a time when you hit that perfect deep serve or spun a return into your opponent's backhand? If you are truly in tune with yourself, you might also hear the click of the ball flying off the paddle, and see the trajectory of the ball flying over the net. The concept of visualization is about creating a mental picture of a situation before it happens.

This workout will highlight different aspects of imagery: What is imagery? Who uses it? When can it be used? How can it be used? And how can it help improve your performance on the court?

I use imagery as a key mental skill with all athletes I work with. The most important component when beginning to use imagery is that the person is relaxed, centered, and calm. Before we start, we usually settle in and take a few breaths.

What is imagery? Imagery is the purposeful act of mentally rehearsing a task with the intent of learning it. When athletes use imagery, they create a blueprint of the shot, incorporating all of the senses: visual, kinesthetic, auditory, tactile, and olfactory. Additionally, it involves imagination, emotion, feelings, and moods.

Essentially, the idea is to use your imagination to create or recreate a situation in the future, which will help you prepare for any possible scenario. For example, while being up 10-9 in a pickleball game, a pickleball player may visualize themselves taking their time, rehearsing their serve routine, and hitting the ball to their intended target.

Who uses imagery? All top athletes do. I suspect that you have even used it—it is almost impossible not to have done so at some point. Have you ever imagined receiving a present, eating your favorite food, or going out with a friend? Have you ever studied for a test by running scenarios through your mind, planning out the best way to solve a problem? Most people use imagery in their day-to-day life without even knowing it. Imagine what would happen if you incorporated it intentionally into your day-to-day practices? If you are like most athletes, it will be beneficial.

When can imagery be used? Imagery can be used to practice certain shots, mechanical adjustments, rituals, or situations that a pickleball player is trying to incorporate into their game. Maybe you want to learn a different technique that allows you to hit a serve deeper or speed up a shot in the kitchen. It can also be used to prepare for the unexpected situations that are likely to present themselves during a tournament. This may include imaging various challenging situations that you may encounter during a game, and visualizing how you will handle them. Such situations may include a bad bounce, sun in your eyes, or even your opponent making a bad call. You can use visualization to imagine a situation before it happens and craft your response by seeing yourself remaining calm and centered while dealing with adversity.

How can imagery be used? Picture a pickleball player's game that you admire and would like to model. Specifically, identify the characteristics and attributes of that player that make them unique, and envision yourself possessing those same attributes. For instance, take Ben Johns' ability to drive the ball straight to targeted areas in singles. Visualize yourself playing with the skills you believe make him great. You will become empowered as you see yourself playing with calm, skill and confidence.

How will getting comfortable using imagery help you improve your performance? It's easy! Practice imagery for five minutes a day. The body's central nervous system doesn't differentiate between the actual event and imagery, so practicing imagery on its own can be helpful. Even better, visualize any shot, technique, or situation which you are hoping to improve. This programs your nervous system to have already experienced the emotions of that shot or situation. With enough practice, you will become more comfortable with the skill or situation.

The A, B, C's to the mental game...

- *Accept*
- *Breath*
- *Concentrate*

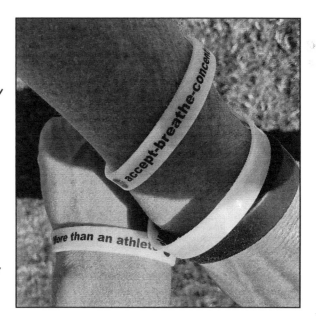

Dream On!

Self-Guided Imagery Script

(Instructions: read the script slowly, and pay attention
to what you experience as you read the words)

Find a comfortable position...and be aware of the sounds around you. Take them in...and notice your breathing...Just observe its natural rhythm...without judging yourself, your thoughts, or your feelings...Simply notice them for the moment...and let them float by...allowing yourself this moment of quiet...You may begin to notice your body slowing down...and feeling your body unwind...just let it unfold...and observe this natural pendulum...

Now, would it be okay to turn your attention inward?...I wonder if you can take yourself to a special place...a place where you feel comfortable and secure...a place we will call 'Inside Your Zone'...in this place...you're relaxed...it can be a place you have visited before...or a place you can only go via your imagination...it can be a place in your body, or even a feeling somewhere deep inside...that brings comfort...and peace...it can be a combination of all these things...or anything else...know one thing: ...this is your zone...and no one else's...As you look around...notice your surroundings...the smells...and the feel...let it unfold...

With this feeling of being 'Inside Your Zone',...shift your attention to the court...just notice what you see...and let it unfold...in front of you...bring your awareness to a time when you played great...a time when you did your best...be aware of the experience...feel it unfold...notice your energy...and your confidence...from inside YOUR zone...

What's it like to do your best...to put it all on the line...to play from your heart...would it be okay to stay with this feeling...and even make some space for it...just notice what happens...

Now, gently bring attention to your breathing...Know that you can go back to Your zone...any time you want...keep in mind you have the super player inside...and you have the energy inside...use it...tap into it...

When you are ready…slowly bring yourself back…be aware of what your feet feel like touching the floor…and notice the sounds around you…gently open your eyes…

How do you feel now? _____

_____

_____

_____

Look out into the ocean…Simply observe what you experience in your body… When you're nervous during a game, it can be helpful (between points) to bring up a time when you were calm.

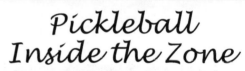

Pickleball
Inside the Zone

PICKLEBALL
ZONE
INSIDE THE

Section 2
PRE-MATCH WORKOUTS

Pre-Game Workouts

Inside the Zone Rap

YoYo, checkit, checkit, checkit check it out
Listen up this is what its about
What I'm gonna say hold big time clout
You're inside the zone, there ain't no doubt

My names is Robbie the rapman
No I'm not dan or even stan
But I'm the man, with the mental training
plan

This is our secret, its got to be
When I rap like this it makes me tree
Its unfiltered expression coming from
inside of me

When you're inside the zone, you feel like
a king on a throne
The look in your opponent's eyes says
they're feeling alone
You gotta trust your instincts, remember
your training
When you're playin' like this, your game
be reigning

It feels like butter, you just let it flow
As it unfolds, you do nothing but glow
When your game's like this you know the feeling
There ain't no ceiling, you're doing the dealing

No thoughts in your head, you're as calm
as can be
Swinging like a butterfly, stinging like a bee
Your movements are smooth, just like water
Playing like this, it's gonna be a slaughter

So remember the day when you did nothing
but play
You dominated the courts and served them on a
lunch tray
When push comes to shove, you gotta play like
a kid
There's so much inside you, open up the lid

— **Rob Polishook**, Author

Workout 10
Mental Principles

- Everyone gets nervous.

- If you are not nervous, you're not human.

- Nerves can be positive and an indicator of passion, they also can help a player prepare.

OMG!...I'm Nervous!
Five Ways to Work Through Pre-Game Jitters

It's Not About Winning or Losing

It's not about winning or losing or better or worse

It is about understanding the journey, a process of developing and improving.

It's not about winning or losing or better or worse, it is about playing the best you can, at any given moment. It is about digging deep and doing your best.

It's not about the past, or the future, it's not about expectations, leave them all at the door. It is about you, playing within yourself, and not trying to do anything more.

It's not about playing the perfect game, there is no such thing, it is about developing a rhythm, breathing and competing. The rest will follow.

It's not about beating your opponent, it is about controlling what you can control, and letting go of what you can't.

It's not about pushing and pulling, rather accepting yourself, noticing what comes up, observing it, and just letting it fly away like a cloud.

It's not about hitting winning shots, or even shots your opponent can't reach. It is about choosing targets, letting your body trust its training and instincts.

Ultimate victory is in the playing, the moment, the thrill, the pursuit, the effort, and the knowing you did everything you could to compete from preparation to the end.

—**Rob Polishook**, author

OMG!...I'm Nervous!

Buzz, Buzz. My phone rings, signaling a new incoming call. Often, it's a Saturday morning, and I might have just finished watching a segment on ESPN while drinking my morning coffee. Or maybe, I have returned from playing pickleball. No matter the scenario, I'm usually pretty relaxed. However, for the caller on the other end, the scene could be very different. They might be a fellow pickleball player with butterflies fluttering in their stomach and their head spinning with possible performance outcomes. Self-doubt might be creeping in, disrupting their peace of mind.

The player may wonder what is happening to them. Why are they feeling this way? Perhaps, they are obsessing about an upcoming match or upset about a loss that they believe should never have happened. It is at this very moment that our paths connect through that Buzz on the cell phone or a short direct text message. The message is always the same: "I'm nervous—what can I do?"

As a mental training coach, the most commonly asked question I receive is how to deal with nervousness before a game. As many players who have experienced such jitters can attest, it's usually not the nervousness itself that presents the problem but rather all the thoughts that accompany it. For example, "Why am I nervous?" or "What happens if I'm still

this nervous when the game begins?" This then sets off another negative spiral, and the player's natural nervousness turns into far more debilitating anxiety.

With this in mind, I would like to share five ideas that can help a nervous pickleball player gain some perspective over what they are experiencing and better manage excessive nervousness prior to a game.

1. It's okay to be nervous.

It's perfectly normal and natural. Being able to accept your nerves is actually the best way to manage them. The top players in any sport don't fight the tension; rather they accept it as "a part of themselves." How many of you have tried to resist a feeling or thought? What happens? It usually becomes more intense and continues to loom in the back of your mind.

2. Nervousness is a sign that you care.

It is neither good nor bad; it simply exists as your unique way of reacting to different situations throughout a game or a tournament. When you are nervous, it's easy to focus only on the negative aspects of how you feel. However, as a player, nervousness can also be a signal that you are excited, challenged, and even focused because you have a great opportunity in front of you. Maybe you're contending late in a game that you've imagined yourself being in since you started playing. So, embrace this challenge. Your nerves are simply a by-product of the thrill.

3. If you are nervous, so are your opponents.

When a pickleball player feels nervous, their focus is usually entirely on themselves, and they don't see the entire picture. They are merely seeing a small piece of it. But do not forget about your opponents! The other players on the court account for the rest of the puzzle. In fact, that opponent you are playing is usually just as nervous as you are, perhaps even more so!

4. Be your best, not "the" best!

Keep the focus on what you can control, such as your effort, energy, and attitude. Being your best will give you the best chance to play well and as a result give you the best chance to win. You can control what you do, strategies you choose, how you bounce back, and taking the time necessary to settle down. The best path to being the best, is to first be your best!

5. Why am I nervous?

When I ask that question to pickleball players, their usual response is "I want to win," or "I don't know how I'm going to do." It's important to understand their focus is distracted from what they can control. They are focusing on the future, winning, which is an uncontrollable result, and on their opponent, which is also uncontrollable. At times, a player may focus on their opponent's previous record or their seeding. Once you shift your focus to the uncontrollable, it leaves little time to focus on what you can control and what you need to do to perform your best.

To summarize, nervousness is a natural emotion and a part of who you are. The problem is not in the nervousness that a pickleball player may experience, but in their negative reaction to it. The next time you are nervous, refer to the five ideas mentioned in this chapter to help shift your focus and play your best game.

OMG!...I'm Nervous!

It's important to understand that everyone experiences nerves. In fact, if you're not nervous, you're probably not human! The reason you feel nervous is that you care and you want to perform well, which is certainly understandable! Moreover, if you're nervous, there is a good chance your opponents are feeling the same way. So, maybe it's okay to be nervous!

Recall a game in which you felt nervous but eventually had a great outcome. Please describe it.

_____

_____

_____

_____

What were you feeling? _____

_____

_____

_____

What did you notice about the nerves as the round went on? _____

_____

_____

_____

What would your experience be if you didn't judge the nervousness as good or bad? _____

_____

_____

Applying the principles discussed in this chapter, what could you use to manage your nervousness? _____

_____

_____

_____

What benefits would you experience if you applied at least one of these principles? _____

_____

_____

_____

Workout 11
Mental Principles

- Your breath is always in the present moment.
- Focus on your breath—calm on the inside, aware on the outside.
- Notice your breath and let go of everything else.

How Do I Play in the Moment?
It's as Easy as Breathing

ON COURT DRILL
Breathing

Purpose: The drill's objective is to become aware of the rhythm in rallies by aligning it with your breath. Focusing on your breath takes the excess tension off of playing a point . The idea is to play points in a non-judgment manner.

Drill:
- Both players position themselves at the kitchen.
- Initiate a back-and-forth exchange of dinking.
- Exhale as you strike the ball.
- Inhale when your opponent strikes the ball and it travels to you.
- Ensure a consistent rhythm throughout.

Progressions:
- Players can shift to the baseline for groundstroke practice and employ the identical breathing practice. Exhale before making contact with the ball. Inhale as the ball approaches you.
- Alternatively, one player can stay at the kitchen and the other player remains stationed at the baseline.

Mental Intention: The objective is for both players to direct their attention towards their breath, quieting mental distractions, technical considerations, and judgments. Establishing a connection with the breath serves to ground players and fosters a state of relaxation, enabling shots to be executed with a natural flow. Even in the event of a missed ball and a temporary pause in the drill, it's important for both players to sustain their focus on their breath. In essence, they continue to breathe while actively engaging in pickleball.

How to Play in the Moment

As you read this, you are breathing. Yet, we often take this subtle, automatic action for granted. Why? Breathing is regulated by our autonomic nervous system, occurring without conscious awareness. By bringing attention to your breath, it can calm you, slow you down, and help you attain a present state of mind—focused, centered, and relaxed.

Our minds can often wander to two places: the past and the future. When our minds are focused on the past, we tend to dwell on memories that have stayed with us, such as a missed shot or a lost game. Similarly, when our minds drift into the future, we may become preoccupied with expectations of what we hope will happen, like winning the next point. However, fixating on either the past or the future can lead to mental errors in the present moment. Both are beyond the control of a pickleball player. To excel, players must remain focused on the present moment, preparing for their next shot.

Fortunately, our body and breath are always in the present, the here and now. The term "present" itself signifies a gift, as being in the present moment is truly precious! Our breath, in particular, is one of the greatest gifts of all. When utilized as an anchor, it helps us stay centered and focused. Simply directing our attention to the natural rhythm of our breath can shift our focus from stressful situations, connecting us to our body, its rhythm, and its innate timing.

Try this experiment: Ask yourself, "Am I breathing?" Sit silently for 30 seconds and notice what happens. Usually, you will find yourself becoming more aware and slowing down. The following three breathing practices can guide you to stay centered, focused, and in a state of calm awareness. Practice them off the court. Then, use the one that feels best for you between shots, games, or whenever you feel your focus slipping.

1. Unguided Breathing.

The object here is to bring your attention to your natural breathing in the present moment. Simply be aware of one of the following senses: sound, feel, or rhythm. How does your breath sound? How does it feel? Notice its rhythm at that moment. Avoid trying to change or judge it. Just observe its natural, organic pace. After five or ten seconds, you will likely notice your breath slowing down, as well as the pace of the game.

2. Word Association Breathing.

As you inhale, say to yourself the words relaxation, slow, or patient, and imagine what it would feel like to embody each of those qualities. Then, as you exhale, say the words anxious, furious, rushing, and imagine letting go of those feelings.

Visualize tension leaving your body, and feel your internal clock aligning to just the right speed. You can create your own words that resonate with your situation, but the key is to inhale what you want to embrace and exhale what you want to let go of.

3. Rhythmic Breathing.

The goal here is to establish a breathing rhythm that feels optimal for you. It's important to find a pattern that works for you and consistently stick to it. You can try inhaling to the count of three, holding your breath for two counts, and then exhaling to the count of four. Just like when a pickleball player is 'in the zone' and consistently makes their shots, finding a rhythm is key. The idea is to discover your own breathing rhythm that feels most natural and effective for you. Feel free to be creative and experiment with different rhythms. Have fun with it!

Whatever breathing practice you choose, once you are centered with a soft focus on your breath, allow your eyes to wander and your attention to expand, taking everything in around you. Be aware of sights and thoughts as they pass by. Metaphorically, this breathing practice is similar to the eye of the hurricane: you are calm on the inside but observant and responsive on the outside.

Slowing down a game with your breath allows you to respond to each shot or tournament with clarity. Remember: clarity creates consistency, and consistency is the key to success in the game!

Mind Full   vs   Mindful

Play present in the here and now!

How to Play in the Moment

It's as Easy as Breathing!

Breathing is regulated by our autonomic nervous system: It happens without conscious thought (fortunately!). By bringing attention to our breath, it helps connect us to our ever-present body.

Below are three different breathing exercises that can be used anytime you need to slow down, shift your focus, and calm down.

Unguided Breathing Exercise

Begin this exercise by asking yourself, "Am I breathing?" Then, simply observe your natural inhalations and exhalations. Take one breath at a time, and notice the sound, sensation, and rhythm, depending on which sense resonates with you the most. Just be aware of this experience and approach it with curiosity. Notice how you may let go of everything else as you focus on your breath.

Word Association Breathing Exercise

List characteristics, attributes, or emotions you would want to **breathe in** and *breathe out*.

PATIENCE	FEAR
Breathe in: _____	Breathe out: _____
Breathe in: _____	Breathe out: _____
Breathe in: _____	Breathe out: _____

Now, as you inhale, imagine how it would feel to breathe patience in, to sense patience flowing through your body. Then visualize breathing out fear, and see it dissipating like a cloud in the wind. Repeat this process with words that resonate with you personally.

Rhythmic Breathing Exercise

Inhale and count how many seconds your breath lasts. Then, observe any possible pause before exhaling and take note of the duration of your exhalation. Explore and discover your own rhythm. What feels most comfortable to you?

Beats in: _____   **Beats holding breath:** _____   **Beats out:** _____

Summary

These three breathing exercises are designed to assist athletes in slowing down, shifting focus, and staying present. Experiment with each exercise to determine which ones you can incorporate into your pre-round, during-round, and post-round routines.

Workout 12
Mental Principles

- Change starts with awareness.
- You are where you are—play in the moment.
- Trust your process.

Court Awareness
Playing With Your Mental Positioning System (MPS)

ON COURT DRILL
Block and Reset

Purpose: The aim of this drill is to practice reset volleys while facing pressure. Reset volleys can prove advantageous during a kitchen firefight, enabling a player to slow the point down and change pace. This shift in rhythm often catches opponents off guard.

Drill:
- One player positions themselves inside the kitchen, right at the net.
- The other player hand-feeds 10 balls to the first player's forehand and another 10 to their backhand.
- The hand-feeding is done from a spot 2 feet behind the first player's kitchen.
- The player at the net focuses on resetting (blocking) the hand-fed balls back into the kitchen.

Progressions:
- Progression 1:
  - The player stationed at the net moves back to their kitchen line.
  - They proceed to execute the same reset volleys, aiming for their opponent's kitchen.
- Progression 2:
  - In the final stage of hand-feeding progressions, the player hitting the volleys relocates to the transition zone.
  - They receive 10 balls in this position.
  - The objective remains dropping the ball into their opponent's kitchen.
- Progression 3:
  - After attaining comfort with the hand-fed drills, the players should replicate the three progressions.
  - This time, the drills are performed with live ball hitting instead of hand-feeds.

Mental Intention: Similar to third shot drops, the reset volley demands patience and enables players to swiftly transition from defense to neutral or from neutral to offense. Often, opponents anticipate a speed-up or an ongoing exchange, so when a ball is reset, the entire tempo of the point shifts.

Court Awareness

Let's flashback 10 years ago to a time when people used to read maps to determine how to reach their destinations. There were three necessary steps: first, you needed to be aware of your current location; second, you needed to know where you wanted to go; and third, you needed to plan the most efficient route to reach your desired destination.

In today's day and age, map reading has been replaced with access to global positioning systems (GPS) in our cell phones or cars. Certainly, the GPS application has made it easier to reach your destination than ever before. All that is necessary is to input the destination, and voilà—the GPS tells you exactly where to go and how to get there. There is no need for much awareness of your current location, and no thinking or planning is required. So, what does this have to do with pickleball? Well, everything...please stay with me.

Clearly, on the pickleball court, we cannot rely on our GPS to help us make adjustments or reach our goals. Thankfully, however, all players do have a similar yet superior tool called cognition. This tool is what I refer to as the MPS, or Mental Positioning System. The MPS is a human machine run by the most powerful computer in the universe; not an electronic device, but our own brain. The MPS is activated by awareness, and it requires us to examine the same three key points

we need to consider when using a map: where we are at this exact point in time, where we want to end up, and what the necessary steps are in order to reach that goal.

Fortunately, a pickleball player can employ their MPS in both practice, recreational play, and tournaments. Once aware, the player's MPS can tell them where they are in a particular situation and what adjustments or steps need to be taken.

Some pickleball players may use their MPS more than others and consequently reap the benefits, while others may take the shortcuts that our GPS uses. For example, many players simply say, "I want to win"—in other words, they input their GPS destination without any awareness of where they are or what steps are necessary to win. Your MPS empowers you to walk your unique path in a thoughtful and direct way. Using the MPS may take longer, but it's the only path to improvement, growth, and consistency. Taking the shorter GPS route will result in inconsistent outcomes because you're essentially throwing spaghetti against the wall, hoping something will stick.

During a tournament, it is imperative to be aware and realize that each situation changes shot by shot and point by point. Because of this, it is key to understand your own tendencies and patterns. This will enable you to make small but important adjustments to your process. For example, imagine you and your partner are playing against a team that mainly hits drives. By recognizing this, you can neutralize their power by hitting soft dinks and forcing them to generate power off shots with little pace that land in the kitchen. From my experience, many comebacks happen simply by a team using their MPS and adjusting their game plan. However, this only works if the team knows what they are doing and where they are.

To use your MPS properly in practice, ask yourself these questions:

- Where am I now, with regard to a particular skill?
- Where do I want to be in a certain amount of time?
- To get there, what do I have to do? What will it take?
- Am I willing to put in an effort to do this? Who can help me?
- How will I know when I reach this goal?

Focus on the ball!

To use your MPS during a game ask yourself these questions:

- What is happening at this moment?
- What do I want to happen?
- What adjustments do I need to make?
- How would a situation change if I made these adjustments?
- What's one adjustment I can make now?

Remember to tune into your internal MPS. Be aware and objectively assess your positioning. This will help you to make the best possible choices and decisions while playing. You will find that using your MPS in point situations is not only empowering but also helps you adapt and adjust during your game.

Court Awareness

You can't get somewhere without being aware of where you are! Try completing the following three steps in regard to a goal or challenge.

Describe where you currently are in regard to a goal or challenge. This is similar to your GPS recognizing where you are. _____

_____

_____

_____

_____

Describe where you want to be in regard to a goal or challenge. This is similar to entering your destination address. _____

_____

_____

_____

_____

Knowing where you are now and where you want to be … what three things do you need to do to get there? This is similar to your GPS displaying the route.

1. _____

2 _____

3. _____

Workout 13
Mental Principles

- Fact: a game is different than practice.
- The more you "need" to win, the less you will.
- Practice the process. Immerse yourself in it.

Why Can't I Play Games Like I Practice?
Five Reasons This Happens

Sport's Paradoxes

- The more you "need" to win, the less you will — "needing to win" adds extra pressure.
- Wanting to win is great…however…what are the steps you need to take to prepare and win?
- Work less and achieve more? — Rest is part of training, not an afterthought.
- Use your goals to motivate you, then in competition let go and just play — Plan with your brain, Play from your heart.
- You can't control the future — But you can prepare for it.
- Change and turnarounds start with awareness — Rock bottom is sometimes necessary for a player to experience and learn from: The sun rises after the darkest hour.
- You often learn more from losses than you can from winning — Failure is feedback, what did it teach you for next time.
- Anyone can win when they're playing well— The secret is competing when you are not at your best.
- Have faith, you may not know it, but you're closer than you think — 211 degrees is hot water, 212 degrees is boiling, steam, locomotion!
- In true competition, no one player is defeated — Both benefit by their efforts to overcome the obstacles presented by the other. Achievement becomes easier when you put less pressure on yourself — If you are afraid to lose…you probably will.
- Crisis = Opportunity — At the heart of every crisis lies a tremendous opportunity. Great things lie ahead for the one who knows the secret to finding opportunity within each crisis.
- Play better by thinking less — Trust yourself and your game, let the game come to you — Remember your training-trust your instincts .

Why Can't I Play Games Like I Practice?

"Why can't I take my practice game to the court?" It's probably the second most frequently asked question I hear, surpassed only by some variation of "I'm nervous, what should I do?" Sometimes this question is uttered as a defiant statement, with the player stubbornly asserting, "If I hit the ball like I do in drills, I would put myself in better positions during my games." Interestingly, this statement is usually true. However, practice and games differ in terms of intensity and pressure.

In practice, whether at the courts with a drilling partner or a foursome, we typically compete against ourselves to improve our own game. However, in a game, there are additional components that can serve as distractions, such as opponents. But what if you thought of them as partners instead of enemies? Yes, as allies who can help you improve, make you uncomfortable, and provide opportunities to learn from adversity.

This workout will explore five key reasons why pickleball players may perform differently in practice compared to games.

1. Loss of Focus.

During a game, a pickleball player's focus is often on the outcome rather than the present moment. When a player fixates on the result of a poor return or returning a speedup, they are directing their attention to something beyond their control. However, when they remain present, they enter problem-solving mode and give themselves the opportunity to evaluate and understand what's important in the current moment. They can also identify areas of their game that require on-court adjustments or changes in strategy. In practice, the focus is usually on the process, such as staying low, selecting targets, and maintaining stillness. During a tournament, it's crucial to let go of the result and shift back to focusing on the process and the elements that are emphasized in practice.

2. Unrealistic Expectations.

During tournaments, many players expect to always perform at their best. Some players have little tolerance for themselves when they hit a less than perfect shot. However, these same players usually anticipate making mistakes in practice and view them as opportunities for learning. In fact, mistakes are a crucial part of skill development. Essentially, pickleball players who allow themselves to fail and then learn from their mistakes put themselves in a better position to achieve their goals. It's important for pickleball players to anticipate making mistakes during competition. Instead of dwelling on a missed serve or a mistake, they should focus on the process of making adjustments, just as they would in practice. This mindset is essential for consistent performance on the pickleball court. Remember, mistakes are inherent in the game, as without them, every shot would be a winner. What matters is how you handle those mistakes, learn from them, and move forward, which will set you apart from your competition.

3. Poor Time Management.

During practice, pickleball players often rush through drills, leaving little time to incorporate routines or discuss the intent of the drill with their drilling partner. It is important to take your time during practice and ensure that the drill is targeting the specific aspect you want to work on in a game. For example, if your intention is to practice reset volleys from the transition zone, make sure the feeds start on a fly and don't rush to the kitchen after the first shot. Instead, consider practicing the transition volley three times before making the drill live to play the point. Utilize specific drills as a way to expose yourself to different situations that you may face in games and tournaments. Practice your process, routines, and rituals before each serve or return. If you like to step away from the ball and take a deep breath, then do so during practice as well. This built-in similarity will help bridge the gap between practice, games, and tournaments for pickleball players.

4. Nerves.

Pickleball players are rarely nervous in practice because they are not judging themselves, and neither is anyone else. However, during a game, players tend to find themselves focusing on the judgment of spectators, their partner, or other players. As a result, they start worrying about the outcome of their oncourt execution, with their attention on uncontrollable factors in the game. It's essential to remember that if you are nervous, so are the opposing players! Nerves are normal at every level.

5. Trying to Impress Others.

During practice, players focus on improving their skills. However, during recreational games and tournaments, when there are others watching, players often lose focus on their process and start worrying about impressing the observers. They may start thinking about showcasing certain aspects of their game, such as attempting a big serve in a crucial situation. A smart pickleball player, on the other hand, will prioritize playing B.A.D.! Yes, you heard that right B.A.D.! This stands for Basics All Day, which includes high percentage shots, staying low, dinking when in trouble, and employing other effective strategies. It's crucial for pickleball players to recognize when they lose their focus and refocus as quickly as possible on the present moment.

Why Can't I Play Games Like I Practice?

In martial arts, there is no differentiation between practice and matches as everything is referred to as practice. This same concept applies to yoga as well. The underlying point is that the focus is always on continuous improvement and striving to get better. So, even though recreational games and tournament matches may differ from practice, what if you viewed everything as a practice? A space for learning and growth!

List three things that you focus on in practice...

1. _____

2. _____

3. _____

When you focus on these things, what do you notice? _____

_____

_____

_____

_____

List three things that you focus on during a game... _____

1. _____

2. _____

3. _____

When you focus on these things, what do you notice? _____

_____

_____

_____

_____

What is the main difference? _____

_____

_____

_____

_____

What things would make sense to let go of when you play your next game? _____

_____

_____

_____

_____

What are some things that would make sense to let go of when you play your next game? _____

_____

_____

_____

Workout 14
Mental Principles

- The outcome is not something you can control.
- Focusing on uncontrollables creates tightness.
- Everyone loses focus. Recognize when this happens and re-focus.

Concentrate!
Focus on What You Can Control

The Archer

When an archer is shooting for nothing, he has all his skill.

If he shoots for a brass buckle, he is already nervous.

If he shoots for a prize of gold, he goes blind or sees two targets. He is out of his mind. His skill has not changed.

But the prize divides him. He cares.

He thinks more of winning than of shooting.

And the need to win drains him of power.

—Chuang Tzu

Concentrate!

We have all heard the phrase, 'He/she lost their focus!' It happens when a pickleball player experiences a lapse in concentration, leading to missed opportunities, such as an easy put-away or a return. It's a common occurrence for most players. One moment, you may feel completely focused, with a smooth, relaxed, and in-control demeanor, and then suddenly, boom! The next moment, you find yourself walking off the court, bewildered, not knowing what happened, as your mind was dwelling in the past or anticipating the future. It can feel like being thrust into another reality, where tension mounts, and every step seems burdensome, as if a weight is pressing down on your back.

Or maybe you've encountered a similar scenario in a different context: You're just one point away from winning the game, and the only thought racing through your mind is, 'I need to get this point.' You start to feel the pressure mounting. Your heart rate increases, and you rush your serve. Before you know it, you find yourself in a crosscourt dink exchange, feeling as though a noose is tightening around your neck, and you're left wondering how your concentration shifted from 'one shot at a time' to being scattered everywhere except the present moment.

Concentration is a crucial yet often misunderstood mental skill. While the dictionary defines concentration as giving something undivided attention or narrowing focus, these definitions may not fully capture the complexity of concentration in the context of competitive sports. Athletes need to develop an action plan and, more importantly, apply it effectively to their specific sport and the various situations they encounter.

Sports psychologist Harvey Dorfman once wisely said, 'To focus on matters beyond our control is to misdirect energy, waste time, and doom us to frustration and failure.' His in-sight suggests that while a pickleball player may be concentrating, if their focus is misplaced, it can actually hinder their performance. It's possible for a player to be concentrating, but not on the right thing. This commonly given advice may not be specific enough. For instance, a player might find themselves reflecting on a previous shot or anticipating the next point, when their focus should actually be on the current shot

My mentor, Dr. Alan Goldberg, a nationally renowned mental training coach, defines concentration as 'the ability to focus on what's important and let go of everything else.' This definition implies that an athlete's concentration may be ineffective if it's directed towards the wrong things. Expanding on Dr. Goldberg's definition, we can further define concentration as 'the choice to focus on what you can control and let go of what you can't control.' Have you ever found yourself fixating on something outside of your control? Reflect on that situation. How did it impact your anxiety levels? How did it affect your concentration when you were standing at the line, ready to serve? Focusing on factors beyond our control almost always derails our performance, creating a sense of helplessness and unease that can lead to a downward spiral. On the other hand, directing our focus towards what we can control, such as our energy level, attitude, and reactions to tournament situations, can boost our confidence and give us more control over our destiny.

There is a helpful strategy that pickleball players can use to enhance their concentration on what they can control before each tournament. Try this exercise: on the left side of a sheet of paper, list the behaviors and strategies that you can control during a tournament and label it as 'controllables.' Your list might include preparation, staying positive, making adjustments, regulating your breathing, managing your reactions to certain situations, or bouncing back from adversity. On the right side of the paper, list what you are unable to control, such as weather, court conditions, or the outcome (as you cannot directly control winning or losing). By simply labeling what you can and cannot control, you will increase your awareness of where you want your focus to be.

For example, a pickleball player cannot control the wind, but they can control how they react to it and make necessary adjustments to ensure their third shot drop has enough power to clear the net. Without this awareness, a player may continue to focus on the wrong things.

With an understanding of what you can and cannot control, it is important to note that an athlete will inevitably lose focus. Rather than getting angry at oneself, the key response is simple: bring your attention back to what you can control. This non-judgmental process will help the athlete shift their focus. Without this awareness, a pickleball player may continue to focus on the wrong things. During games, the choice to refocus on what you can control is equally important as maintaining your focus in the first place.

Another element of proper concentration is to understand that maintaining a strong focus on something 100% of the time is not always necessary. In fact, it can be exhausting and may even lead to burnout. Knowing when to let go and release your focus is important, oftentimes you can do this between points or games. However, the key is to then refocus on what's important. The next point or game! This little focus break can help you to settle down.

In summary, when viewing concentration through the lens of what you can control and what you cannot, it becomes more manageable to perform at your best.

Concentrate!

Concentration: kan(t)•sen•'tra•shen: noun:

A. the act or process of concentrating; the state of being concentrated; especially: direction of attention of a single object.

B. to bring or direct towards a common object. To draw together and meet in a common center; to focus one's power, efforts or attention.

How would you define concentration in the context of sports? _____

_____

_____

Inside the Zone definition of concentration: *The ability to focus on what is important, and let go of everything else.*

Translation:

The ability to focus = The choice to focus

on what is important = on what you can control

and let go of everything else = and let go of what you can't control

New complete definition (write it in): _____

_____

_____

_____

_____

What percentage of the time during a game do you concentrate on what you can control? _____

And what percentage of the time during a round do you concentrate on what you cannot control? _____

Name a time during a game when you were concentrating on the right thing:

_____

What was the result? _____

Name a time during a game when you were concentrating on the wrong thing:

_____

What was the result? _____

_____

Understanding this new definition of concentration, and the above, how could this change things for you? _____

_____

_____

_____

_____

Workout 15
Mental Principles

- Routines help an athlete feel prepared.
- Routines create a sense of familiarity.
- Routines allow the athlete to have control over a situation.

Routines That Work
Plan and Prepare for the Next Tournament

Routines and Strategies That Work

Return and run to the kitchen

Serve and stay back (until you hit a 3rd shot drop or drive)

Stay low when at the kitchen (and all shots)

Set a stable base when hitting the ball

If the ball is high, let it fly (out)

Hit third shot drops to opponents backhand

Hit drives and drops to the middle

Hit serves and returns deep

Doubles partners move together

Aim for your opponent's feet

Eliminate excess movement and keep all shots compact

Paddle in front, avoid large backswings

Routines That Work

You cannot control the future, but you can prepare for it. I love this saying because it reminds us of an important concept before a big tournament. Most pickleball players have heard about routines, but what can you do 24 to 36 hours before the tournament? The answer is: a lot! It is important to understand that this is not the time to make technical swing changes. Instead, mental preparation is key.

Think of it this way—if you were a pilot, you would have a checklist of all the things you needed to double-check before takeoff. If you were a carpenter, you would "measure twice and cut once." The same goes for sports! The main goal at this point is to be relaxed so that your natural talents, skills, and intuition can flow effortlessly during the competition. Therefore, it's crucial to focus on clearing away potential distractions that may interfere with your performance before you play.

Almost all athletes, both professional and amateur, have routines to prepare themselves for tournaments. These routines help players gain a sense of calm before starting. The rest of this workout will highlight the key actions that should be part of your pre-tournament routine.

1. Pre-Round Checklist and 'Altar'.

The evening before a tournament, it's important to lay out and pack your pickleball bag with everything you'll need for the competition the next day. My wife, Debbie, a marathon runner, calls this process "laying out her altar." It ensures that she has everything necessary to compete and won't have to run around in a panic trying to find something at the last minute. Proper preparation also helps you stay relaxed on the day of the tournament by eliminating the need to complete last minute tasks. Items for the altar might include a towel, the balls that will be used in the tournament, socks, water, snacks, and a hat.

2. Sleep and Hydration.

Hopefully, you've been getting enough sleep and staying hydrated leading up to the tournament. However, it's crucial to get to bed early in the evening before a tournament. Sometimes you might end up playing 8 to 10 games in a day. Most adults need eight hours of sleep for a great rest, while kids usually need ten hours. Plan this into your evening and work backwards to ensure you get enough sleep. I also recommend staying hydrated leading up to the tournament and keeping water by your bed.

3. Stretch and Warm-Up.

This step is often overlooked, but it's crucial. Certain circumstances may prevent you from warming up, which makes stretching even more important. The idea is to warm up your body, get your mind moving, and stay relaxed. One exercise that I love to use is visualizing some of your best shots from your own personal highlight reel. If you're familiar with the court you'll be playing on that day, run through some of your highlights from prior games. This will help you think about your strategy and mentally prepare for the competition. It will also incorporate muscle memory into the mix.

4. Tranquilo.

This step is often ignored, yet it's helpful in achieving a relaxed and balanced mindset. Just before your game isn't the time to concoct new strategies or devise technical adjustments. Many players prepare with their headphones on or by taking a walk to settle in. I recommend stepping away from the courts and focusing on your breath—just slowly and easily being aware of your breath and surroundings. Whatever your technique, find what works to relax your mind.

Utilize these four routines to prepare for success: proper preparation will keep you relaxed before playing, enabling you to stay calm and unleash your natural talent once the game starts!

What if one book could change...

Rob Polishook, M.A., C.P.C.

PICKLEBALL
INSIDE THE ZONE

32 Mental Training Workouts for Champions

EVERYTHING!

Routines That Work

Pre-Round Checklist

Prior to takeoff, a pilot will methodically go through a checklist to ensure the plane is properly equipped with the right supplies and will run smoothly. Similarly, a mentally prepared player will go through their pickleball bag and ensure that everything is in order with the proper supplies for an important game. Improper preparation will immediately put you a step behind.

The first few items are intangible and cannot be put in your bag: only you can control them:

1. A good night's sleep on the nights leading up to your round, especially the evening before (eight hours minimum)!

2. Hydrate your body by drinking water leading up to the tournament

3. Maintain a positive, problem-solving, and happy attitude.

Bag Check:

1. ____Extra balls

2. ____Towel

3. ____Water

4. ____Banana/fruit snacks/PB & J

5. ____Notebook

6. ____Sunglasses/sunscreen

7. ____Extra paddle

8. ____Extra shirt and socks

9. ____Something that makes you smile ☺

10. ____Maybe *PickleBall Inside the Zone*!

Workout 16
Mental Principles

- Beating yourself up is never helpful.
- Nothing changes unless you make a change.
- Being curious, not furious is a more productive approach.

Stay Positive!
Seven Questions for Improvement

Be Grateful

Frequently, we become entangled in the outcomes of a pickleball game. We tend to judge ourselves or make comparisons to previous matches or even the person we're currently playing with. This brief exercise aims to help you recognize three aspects you're grateful for during a drill session or a match.

Prior to commencing play, take a moment to pinpoint something you are grateful for. If you desire, you can share it with your partner. Undoubtedly, you are thankful for playing with them; consider expressing this sentiment. Acknowledge that without their presence, you'd be playing alone. Extend your gratitude by thanking them for being there!

During the midst of a match, take a moment to reflect on something you are grateful for; once more, you can choose to share it with your partner. If you are engaged in drills, express your gratitude for honing a specific aspect of your game. Alternatively, you might simply appreciate playing a game with friends on a beautiful day.

As your session concludes, take a moment to reflect on and/or share something you are grateful for. It might be the satisfaction of feeling good throughout the entire match or drill session. It could also involve the accomplishment of learning or successfully executing a specific shot. Alternatively, your gratitude might stem from the opportunity to share the court with certain players.

Devoting time to express gratitude aids in being present and fully immersed in the moment. This practice, in turn, contributes to slowing down your pace and fostering a sense of centeredness and tranquility. Consequently, whatever unfolds in the subsequent moments, you'll approach it from a place of balance and equanimity.

Stay Positive!

Have you ever played pickleball game after game, day after day, hoping to improve? Or taken lessons and attended clinics, looking for that one technique that will give you the edge you're looking for? Maybe you've watched countless YouTube videos, hoping to glean a few valuable instructional tips. If you answered "yes" to at least one of these questions, you're not alone. But what if I told you that you could further improve your game by asking yourself seven thoughtful questions? Would that be worth it to you?

Below, you'll find seven questions that can help you improve your game through increased awareness, self-reflection, and by setting specific, process-oriented goals. These questions will highlight what's working well in your game, where you want to improve, and the crucial steps to take in between to help you climb to the level you're hoping to reach.

I recommend keeping a journal where you can answer these questions after each time you play. Once you've identified the specific steps you need to take to improve your game, create a practice plan where you can drill cooperatively with a friend and work on those specific. For example, if your third shot drop isn't holding up under pressure, or you're struggling to return an opponent's slice serve, create a drill that simulates those situations and practice that particular shot. If you're getting caught in the chicken wing area on speed-ups from opponents, practice keeping your racket out in front, creating space for the volley, or even keeping the dink away from their forehand.

Regardless of the areas you identify as needing improvement, it's important to approach them from a positive mindset. Ask yourself, 'What am I doing well, and what would be ideal?' This growth-oriented approach allows for positive development and progress. Alternatively, you could choose to take a negative approach and say, 'I stink at everything, nothing is going right, I have to improve everything.' However, this mindset doesn't work, thinking this way can be overwhelming and is counterproductive.

Instead, ask yourself:

- What part of my game is working?
- What is behind my overall success?
- What would my ideal game look like? What shots would I be hitting?
- What is the difference between where my game is now and where I want it to be?
- What specific steps do I need to take to get my game where I want it to be?
- What do I need to do and/or do I need help?
- When can I start working on this?

Stay Positive!

What am I doing in my game that is working? _____

_____

What is behind my overall success? _____

_____

What would my ideal game look like? What shots would I be hitting? _____

_____

What is the difference between where my game is now and where I want it to be?

_____

_____

What steps do I need to take to address these differences? _____

_____

_____

What do I need to do and/or who can help me? _____

_____

_____

When can I start taking action? _____

_____

_____

Pickle and Practice
(Drilling is always a good idea)

PICKLEBALL
ZONE
INSIDE THE

Section 3
MATCH WORKOUTS

Match Workouts

Something Inside You

Not knowing if you're going to win
Is where belief, faith and trust come in.
Belief, faith and trust in self
And in those that believe in you.

There is never a guarantee
Mistakes will happen along the way.
However, learning is part of the process.
Victory is in committing
And putting yourself on the line.

No doubt this is hard to do
Scary and uncertain
Few are in a position to do it
Fewer do it.

However, if you choose to…
What's possible?
What could you learn?
How could you grow?
What could you accomplish?

There are no certain answers…
Along the journey
But faith, belief and trust can guide you…

Learn to listen to that "something inside
  you…"

— **Rob Polishook**, Author

Workout 17
Mental Principles

- A between-point ritual helps you stay centered in what can otherwise be a chaotic moment.

- A between-point ritual helps you stay focused on what you can control.

- A between-point ritual should be personal and meaningful.

Between-Point Rituals
Don't Leave Home Without It!

ON COURT DRILL
Between-Point Rituals

Purpose: To establish a ritual that assists the player in becoming mentally and physically prepared before beginning the next point.

Drill:
- Two or four players participate in a regular game.
- Each player executes the following three-part ritual
- After the point ends:
  1. The player holds their paddle in their non-dominant hand.
  2. They take a few deliberate breaths, inhaling and exhaling.
  3. They vocalize the word "next."
- The subsequent point will only commence once the three-part ritual is concluded.

Progressions: Players have the flexibility to create a short ritual which works for them The pivotal aspect is to identify something that resonates with you as a player, a choice you genuinely wish to employ for resetting. This should not be something you feel obligated to do; otherwise, it would merely become an additional task to complete.

Mental Intention: The concept revolves around ensuring that a player dedicates the necessary time to transition into a state of calmness, centeredness, and focus for the upcoming point. Frequently, players tend to hurry to the next point, overlooking the significance of releasing the previous point and moving on to the next. Conversely, even after winning a lengthy point, players might rush into the next point and make an error. The essential idea is to engage with each point from a foundation of grounded calmness and centeredness. Although the next point will be played, the pivotal question is: will the players be prepared?

Between-Point Rituals

In sports, and in life, athletes are required to perform under pressure. It is part of the game. Think back to a time you experienced a high-pressure situation during your pickleball game. How did you manage it? Imagine that you're playing in the finals against Ben Johns and Ana Leigh Waters, two formidable opponents! How would you handle it?

Whether it's a recreational game, club championship, or even a fun day playing with friends, we always encounter challenges and pressure that come with it. More often than not, high-pressure situations can make us feel tense, anxious, and sometimes hesitant. More importantly, what is your between-point ritual for staying calm and present in these situations?

Between-point rituals are personal processes that each athlete uses to help them stay calm, centered, and prepared for the next shot. This ritual is your opportunity to step back into your bubble where you can control things. It might seem like a small act, but the ritual is extremely empowering for any pickleball player. The between-point ritual takes your mind off of what you cannot control and helps you focus on what you can control.

Your between-point ritual is a valuable tool in a game as well. By utilizing your between-point ritual during a game, you can let go of the previous point and properly prepare yourself for the next one.

The between-point ritual that I teach has four stages:

The first stage is the **acknowledgement stage**, which simply involves making yourself aware of what happened during the previous point, both the good and the bad. Once you're aware of your current situation, you can move on to the next stage and facilitate change.

The second stage is the **centering stage**, where you should focus on your breathing. The purpose is to bring your attention to the present moment and balance your nervous system.

The third is the **strategy stage**, where you decide on your options and determine the best way to approach your next shot.

The last stage is the **physical stage**, which helps you gain control with a familiar action and establish your rhythm.

The bottom line is that competition is full of pressure. A between-point ritual helps us stay calm, centered, and composed. By having your own between-point ritual in place, you can better manage these situations and embrace challenges. The goal of a between-point ritual is to refocus and move beyond stress towards your goals. By creating and implementing a between-point ritual, we can enhance our physical and emotional preparedness, increase our sense of control, and feel more comfortable even in high-pressure situations.

Between-Point Rituals

Name a player whose between-point ritual you like: _____

Describe what their between-point ritual looks like: _____
_____
_____

How do you think it's helpful to them? _____
_____
_____

How could a between-point ritual be helpful to you? _____
_____
_____

Create your own unique between-point ritual: _____
_____
_____
_____
_____
_____
_____

Workout 18
Mental Principles

- Everyone feels fear. It's what you do with it that counts.

- Pressure isn't bad, it just is.

- If it were easy, everybody would be doing it.

Tense, Nervous... Can't Relax?
How to Manage Pressure

ON COURT DRILL
Game Point Pressure

Purpose: The purpose is to provide players with the opportunity to learn how to handle adversity in high-pressure situations, especially when the outcome of the game is at stake.

Drill: The drill involves two to four players.
- One team starts with 10 points (game point), and the other team with 7 points.
- Game Process:
  - The team at game point starts serving.
  - The team winning a point earns serving privilege.
  - Whichever team wins 3 out of 5 is the winner.

Progressions: Players have the choice to initiate the score at any point they desire, mimicking various scenarios and pressures. For instance, they could begin the game at 8-8, and engage in a best-four-out-of-seven games format.

Mental Intention: For both teams, it is crucial to remain present and concentrate on strategy, execution, and resilience. The focus should not be solely on winning the point, as the outcome is beyond their control. The team in the lead should emphasize what is necessary to close out the game, while the team behind can focus on managing the adversity of being behind and striving to mount a comeback.

Tense, Nervous...Can't Relax?

How many times have you heard that the secret to playing your best is by being in the present moment? Have you ever experienced being inside the zone? Conversely, how many times have you experienced being outside of the zone where your thoughts were focused on the past, the future, or even others' expectations of you? For example, you might be preparing to serve, but you're still thinking about the previous point. Have you ever caught yourself playing in the future, where, after winning a game, you fast forward to what happens if you win the match and find yourself in the finals? Surely, whenever you're in the past or in the future, the results are adversely affected. Why is this? It is actually pretty easy to understand. If you're playing in the past or the future, you have one eye on something you can't control and the other on the point. Certainly, this is no recipe for success! Once your attention is divided, your play will suffer.

So, the bigger question becomes: What are some things you can do to help yourself focus on the present task at hand while you're competing? Once you become aware that your focus is in the wrong place, what are some pressure-release practices that you can use to calm yourself, get centered, and bring yourself back to the present moment simultaneously?

Here's the good news! We are all born in the present and have the ability to stay in it and play in it. To remain in the present takes discipline, awareness, and the desire to not attach to counter-productive thoughts, such as missing a key volley or a third-shot drop. Interestingly, sometimes change is more frightening to a player than continuing to spiral out of control. How often have you witnessed a pickleball player continue to miss a shot and not try something new? Hence, the saying goes, 'It may feel good to swim with an anchor, but the weight of it is constantly going to drag you down.'

It's helpful for a pickleball player to use pressure-release practices (PRPs) in tight situations when things seem to be getting out of control. These PRPs are designed to take your mind off the fearful or anxious situation and refocus your attention on the present moment. In this refocused state, you can calmly focus on what needs to be done and play by using your natural, instinctual game instead of overthinking technique, the past, or the future.

The following are four pressure-release practices.

1. Routine.

Routines can be very effective for athletes. They provide a sense of comfort, consistency, and control, allowing for a more singular focus. Serious pickleball players should create a pre-match routine that they can practice the evening before a game.

This routine might include a familiar meal plan, equipment preparation, and some relaxation exercises to help them prepare for the tournament ahead instead of stressing about it. Another recommended routine is deciding what to do pre-serve. This pre-serve routine (see Chapter 17) may include some breath work (described in practice 2 below), designating an area on the court that serves as a positive space, or recalling an inspirational moment where you had success in a previous situation.

2. Breathing.

I strongly advocate using your breath as a centering and calming practice. By bringing your attention to your breath and noticing its sound, feel, or rhythm, you will automatically bring yourself to the present moment. The simple act of doing this, of even asking yourself, "Am I breathing?" will take your mind off the pressure, help you release stress, and bring your attention to the present. There are many different breathing techniques to choose from. Find one that you are most comfortable with. The key here is that your breath is always in the present. Attaching to your breath will help you detach from stress, create a sense of calm, and put you in the best position to play the next shot.

3. Anchors.

An anchor is something to which you can bring your attention, such as a memory, an inspiration, or a designated place on the court that is calming. The key to this practice is that the anchor brings about positive and safe feelings. It may be the feeling of hanging out at the beach or being with a certain someone. The idea is that this anchor is connected to a feeling that facilitates a sense of calm in your body. For instance, the thought of the ocean is often very calming for people. Focusing on this often helps a pickleball player let go, release pressure, and center themselves. Your anchor should be personal to you, and just the thought or vision of it should lead to a sense of warmth, calmness, and safety.

4. Be curious, not furious.

This one may sound funny, but the act of being curious puts you in the present without any preconceived judgments. Being curious creates an awareness of what is happening around you without thoughts of the past or future getting in the way. Try this: instead of being angry or even ecstatic at your result, be curious about what happened. When you are curious, you usually become more in-tune and open to what is going on around you. You will also find yourself becoming less judgmental of the situation, which then allows you to respond in a calmer fashion, rather than merely reacting quickly."

Try these pressure-release strategies and see which ones work best for you. The key to all of these practices is that they allow you to move away from a stressful situation and offer a sense of calm in return.

Tense, Nervous...Can't Relax?

In this chapter, I have addressed ideas that can help you slow down, change your focus, and relax during tense situations (routines, breathing, anchors).

Let's briefly explore what can happen in a tense situation. Oftentimes, a player will describe their heart speeding up, not feeling certain parts of their body, trembling or shaking, and feeling inclined to speed things up. In contrast, players in the zone describe feeling relaxed, with time slowing down, and swinging the paddle effortlessly.

Our energy naturally goes up and down like a wave in the ocean, unless a fear, anxiety, or situation threatens us and causes us to spike up (freeze). It's important to understand that the thought itself is not the problem, but rather our reaction to the thought. For example, if we think "I missed that shot," and then take it a step further to mean "I'm going to lose," that's when we create a problem for ourselves.

When fears and anxiety enter your mind, practice not reacting to them, but rather just being curious about them. Don't add anything to the emotion, just be aware of it. Usually, it will go away on its own.

Anchoring Exercise:

Step 1: Think of a time or experience in a game where you faced adversity but overcame it. Describe it. _____

_____

_____

_____

Step 2: When you think of it, notice how you feel. Describe it. _____

_____

_____

_____

Step 3: Imagine a situation in the future which may make you feel tight or nervous. Describe it. _____

_____

_____

_____

Step 4: Now, imagine the time from Step 1 where you turned things around, just noticing that centered, competent feeling . . . _____

_____

_____

_____

Step 5: What do you notice? _____

_____

_____

_____

Now, go back to the future situation that makes you nervous. You may notice that by changing the focus to a feeling of accomplishment (overcoming adversity), the nervousness of the future event may subside and not be as intense as before.

Workout 19
Mental Principles

- Everyone gets nervous; it's how you manage it.
- Just be You.
- When tense, slow down and notice your *breath*.

Tension, Tears, and Twitches
The Secret to Managing Stress

ON COURT DRILL
Tense and Nervous

Purpose: Enhance your consistency, calmness, and mental clarity during crucial points in high pressure situations.

Drill:
- Two or four players can play. All players stand at the kitchen line.
- Players are only allowed to execute dink shots across the net.
- Dinks can be handled on the bounce or intercepted out of the air.
- Dinks landing 6 inches beyond the non-volley zone are acceptable; these are considered deep pressurized dinks and won't result in point loss.
- Speed-ups are prohibited in this drill.

Scoring Process:
- The player feeding the ball keeps track of the number of times the ball crosses the net.
- If the ball crosses the net 11 times before an error occurs, the winning player is awarded 11 points.
- In scenarios of lengthy dink exchanges, such as 35 hits, the player winning the point obtains the equivalent number of points (35 points in this example).
- Players continue until one individual or team accumulates 100 points or more.

Progressions:
- This game can now be played with speed-ups.
- While points may be briefer, it encourages patience until a real opportunity to speed up or attack arises.

Mental Intention: As a point extends, players frequently experience growing pressure, leading them to either rush the point or attempt an impractical winning shot prematurely. The superior option is to remain patient and then make the appropriate choice. This particular scoring system replicates pressure and aids players in becoming accustomed to extended dink exchanges, fostering composure, and enhancing shot tolerance.

Tension, Tears, and Twitches

How many of you get nervous while waiting to play a game on the challenge court or a tournament? How many of you can feel the pressure as you serve for game point? Nerves play a key role in pickleball and any sport. They can make an athlete physiologically tight. Here is what can happen to a pickleball player when nerves set in: they may get a surge of adrenaline in their central nervous system, their heartbeat may pound hard, beads of sweat may start forming on their skin, their breath may get shorter and shallower, their muscles may contract, and their blood pressure may increase.

Effectively managing pressure is a counter-intuitive process. Rather than ignoring the pressure, it is necessary to accept it. This acceptance neutralizes it and can alleviate the intensity. This is similar to the well-known "elephant in the room" scenario that we all encounter at one time or another. Rejecting, ignoring, or denying that the elephant exists only leads to greater discomfort. Only by acknowledging that stress exists in the mind can we reduce the tension."

A common misconception is that top players don't feel nerves, tension, anxiety, or fear. However, we all experience these emotions, including the top pros. What's important is not fighting our minds to avoid feeling nervous, but accepting that

we are nervous and maintaining our focus on what we can control and what's important at the moment.

There are mental skills that great players utilize to thrive despite such emotions. These players can effectively accept these emotions as part of their individual process and consequently don't attach to them. This allows them to play in a state of focused awareness. How many times have you heard a pickleball player say, "If only I hadn't missed that last third shot drive, I would have won!" The reality is that you cannot separate the mental game from the tactical, technical, and strategic game. They are all interrelated, critical components that surface in high-pressure situations, and top pros know this.

Media, fans, and even players themselves often misunderstand nerves and how to manage them. It is common to hear a statement such as, "champions don't like to admit to nerves." In many cases, this may be accurate, but many elite players are not afraid to express how they experience their emotions.

Professionals and amateurs are often discouraged from being honest about their emotions and are consequently compelled to fight an internal battle to deny what they are feeling. Mind you, it is one thing to openly publicize your nervousness to your opponent, but the real trouble comes when a pickleball player does not privately allow themselves to acknowledge what they are experiencing. When a player fights emotions, their focus stays on the emotional state (inducing concern or panic over what they are suppressing) rather than accepting it for what it is and making the choice to move on. Resisting an emotion's existence only makes it stronger. Think "elephant in the room"!"

In conclusion, a machine-like mentality to ignore nerves is misdirected. In fact, it pushes athletes further from peak performance because they are scared to be themselves and to fully acknowledge their mental and emotional experience. Great athletes instinctively understand a key mental edge secret—it is okay to have nerves. In fact, accepting the experience of tension is the first step towards releasing it.

Sometimes
when things are
falling apart
they may actually be
falling into place

Tension, Tears, and Twitches

The Secret to Managing Stress

When was a time you were feeling stressed or nervous on the court? _____

_____

Does this happen often? _____

What did you do? _____

_____

_____

What are some things you could do to help release the tension and refocus? Hint: Refer to previous chapters for more pressure-release practices; i.e. breathing.

1. _____

2. _____

3. _____

4. _____

5. _____

How could this help you? _____

_____

_____

Workout 20
Mental Principles

- Look at what's happening, not what happened.
- Negative self-talk comes from a part of you that is scared.
- The secret to managing self-talk is to notice it but not get caught up in it.

I SUCK!
How to Tame Negative Self-Talk

ON COURT DRILL
How to Tame Negative Self-Talk

Purpose: The goal is to eliminate judgment on shots and transition smoothly from misses to successful shots, including winners and faults.

Drill:
- Both players position themselves at the kitchen line.
- They engage in dink shot exchanges, creating a rally.
- Upon contacting the ball, each player verbalizes the word "yes."

Progressions:
- Players can engage in this collaborative game by dinking to each other.
- Alternatively, they can apply the same drill using volleys.
- They can further practice by hitting baseline drives to each other.
- Additionally, they have the option to play points.

Mental intention: The goal is to develop a consistent and repeatable rhythm, regardless of whether the ball lands in or out. Often, players might miss a shot, but by maintaining the "yes" mindset, they proceed to the next shot. There's no room for "omg" or any negative self-talk; instead, they say "yes," regardless of the outcome, and transition smoothly to the next shot.

I SUCK!

All competitive players recognize negative self-talk. It starts with that devilish little voice in our head that raises doubts, fears, and questions about our ability to perform. The little voice usually comes during the most pressure-packed times in a game. It's the voice that says, 'I suck! I'm pathetic!' after a missed reset volley or third shot drop, or 'How could you do that again?' after another errant shot. It's that cynical little voice that whispers, 'If you lose the next point, you're going to lose the game,' or 'I'm never going to get better,' after a lost match. Negative self-talk is preceded by negative self-thoughts. Without proper awareness, negative thoughts can bring even the most competitive pickleball player down.

When a player chooses to listen to their negative self-talk and begins a negative self-dialogue, that is when the downward spiral usually begins. It often plays out like this: a player mis-hits a ball that they expected to put away, and in their head, the little voice of doubt enters and begins chiming in. Simultaneously, their body starts to get tight. Instead of moving on to the next shot, stepping back, or any other form of refocusing, the verbal self-talk begins and the player continues to harp on the past, verbally berating themselves. All of this leads to tight muscles, loss of feel, and further errors.

It's important to understand that we have a choice when it comes to reacting or responding to our negative self-talk. When we react defensively and deny its existence, the voice only gets louder. There's a saying: "What you resist, persists." By trying to deny or ignore the voice, we unintentionally give it more power. It's also crucial to recognize that just because we have a negative self-thought doesn't make it true. For instance, have you ever had a negative thought like "It's over; I'm going to lose" when you were on the brink of losing a tournament, only to bounce back? That's because you accepted the thought without judgment, neither validating nor invalidating it. Consequently, the thought faded away, and you could play the game like any other.

So, what can a pickleball player do when they get bombarded with negative self thoughts, especially in the thick of a tight game under pressure? If the pickleball player is aware of the self-thoughts and the patterns, they can make the choice to step away and change their focus. The following six practices can be used when negative self-thoughts start creeping into your head and negative self-talk begins to spew out of your mouth.

1. Be aware and let it dissolve away.

The problem is not the negative thinking—it's normal to experience it in high-pressure situations. Instead of resisting or fighting with these thoughts, simply observe them without judgment. Take a step back, focus on your breath, and visualize the thoughts being released as you exhale

2. Welcome and normalize.

Say "hello" to the negative thoughts— by acknowledging them, you normalize them. You can actually say to thoughts, "Hey, thanks for sharing your concerns but I'm in the middle of a game. Go back to the sidelines." You might also pretend that your favorite comedian is mimicking this reply, which can bring humor to the situation.

3. Put a time limit on it.

Once you notice negative self-talk, give yourself a specific amount of time to dwell on it, and then move on. For example, you could say, "I'm going to allow myself to be frustrated about that shot for 5 seconds, and then I'm going to refocus on the next point." It's important to acknowledge the feeling without getting stuck in it. Don't say, "I stink," but rather, "I made a mistake on that shot." Even after a game ends, it's common for players to come off the court feeling down and saying things like, "I suck." While ideally, the player wouldn't feel this way to begin with, a more realistic and healthier approach would be, "I may not have played my best today, but I can learn from my mistakes and do better next time.

4. Reframe the situation.

Imagine that you are serving to win. You step up to the line and the thought comes up: "Uh oh, I'm so nervous." Ask yourself: "What is another way of looking at this?" How about considering the situation as a challenge instead of a threat? Instead of dwelling on the obstacles associated with our nerves, we can shift our attention to the process that entails what we must do to overcome them.

5. Shift your focus.

When negative thoughts start to overwhelm you, redirect your attention to something else. Focus on your feet or your breath, and approach the situation with curiosity instead of judgment. Taking a brief five-second break from the negative self-talk can help you regain your composure and concentration.

In summary, we all have negative thoughts. However, when they escalate to self-talk, it's important to regain control of the situation. Even the best players experience doubts, fears, and nerves, just like everyone else. The question is how we respond, play through it, and avoid the downward spiral of negativity. When in doubt, go back to the five practices to combat those "I suck" thoughts and regain your focus.

I SUCK!

The Art of Talking to Yourself!

We all talk to ourselves…you know that little inner judgmental critic that says "you shoulda done this," or "you coulda done that." Sometimes the critic even calls you names! "I'm an idiot" or "I can't believe you did that!"

Can you recall a game when you were highly frustrated? _____

Describe the situation: _____

_____

_____

With that round in mind, list all the negative things you thought or said aloud. (Be honest!)

1. _____

2. _____

3. _____

4. _____

5. _____

Looking at this list, what does it make you aware of? _____

_____

How did saying these things affect your confidence and performance? _____

_____

_____

Would you say these things to your best friend? _____

Why not? _____

_____

_____

What could you do to bounce back from the mistakes? _____

1. _____

2. _____

3. _____

How would this be helpful? _____

_____

_____

Leave Your EGO
off the court...
Play with **EGOH** *on the court!*

E - equanimity		
G - gratitude		
O - originality		
H - humility		

Workout 21
Mental Principles

- Expect the unexpected.
- It's inevitable to lose your concentration at times, but what's important is to bring it back to what you can control.
- The most important moment is the NEXT moment.

You Cannot Be Serious!
Seven Tools to Help You Regain Your Focus

ON COURT DRILL
Lost Focus and Regain Focus

Purpose: The "Third Shot Drop Challenge" drill aims to enhance players' third shot drop technique and their capability to neutralize opponents at the net. Furthermore, it contributes to improving consistency and accuracy under pressure.

Drill:
- One player assumes the position at the kitchen (NVZ), while the other stands at the baseline, mimicking the ideal stance for executing a third shot drop.
- The player at the kitchen initiates the drill by starting the feed.
- Both players participate in a rally, with the baseline player focusing on effectively executing third shot drops to neutralize their opponent.
- If the baseline player misses a shot, another ball is introduced, and the cumulative count of successful third shot drops is recorded.
- Conversely, if the player at the kitchen (NVZ) misses a shot, another ball is introduced, and the cumulative count continues for the baseline player.
- The drill continues until the baseline player misses five shots.
- At that juncture, the players switch positions, and the drill is executed in reverse.
- The player with the highest cumulative score of successful third shot drops at the end of the drill is declared the winner.

Progressions: The "Third Shot Drop Challenge" drill is easily adaptable for three or four players.
Three Players Progression:
- Two players position themselves at the kitchen.
- The third player focuses on executing third shot drops.
- Four Players Progression:
- Two players take positions at each kitchen side.
- The other two players focus on hitting third shot drops.

Mental Intention: The primary focus of the "Third Shot Drop Challenge" drill is to develop consistency and repeatability in executing the third shot drop. It is crucial for the player to aim for consistent performance across all balls in the drill.

You Cannot Be Serious!

Even some of the best pickleball players lose their focus during a game. However, they are also known for their ability to regain their focus quickly. Losing focus is not a problem unless it leads to a downward spiral. What's important is to be aware when you lose your focus and refocus on what you can control.

It's one thing to see other players lose their focus, but can you recall a time when you were on the court and lost your focus due to a missed shot that you thought was an easy one? It can be frustrating, but the real challenge is regaining your focus to bring yourself back to a place of calm, where you can play the next point free of distractions.

It's important to recognize when you've lost your focus. It may seem simple or obvious, but awareness is the first step to regaining it. When faced with adversity, you can choose to slow down and refocus. Keep in mind that it takes courage to change your focus and reach a place of calm. To regain your focus and stay on track in challenging situations, try using the following tools:

1. Rituals.

The power of rituals lies in their predictable nature. Pickleball players can rely on them to feel more comfortable during unpredictable situations. For this reason, rituals can help bring you back to a place of calm. They keep players comfortable and in control, and focus their attention on the present moment.

2. Self-coaching.

Pickleball players can use self-coaching to trigger physiological responses by asking themselves questions. For example, you can ask, "How would I feel if I were relaxed?" or "What would it feel like if I were having fun?" or "What would be different if I looked at this situation as a challenge instead of a threat?" Asking these questions can help release tension and bring players back to the present moment.

3. Reframing thoughts.

Reframing your thoughts is similar to self coaching in that it involves assessing the immediate situation and using alternative techniques to stay calm. For example, you may catch yourself thinking, "Oh no, here we go again! I always screw up." Instead of fighting these thoughts, try reframing them. For instance, say something like, "I hear you, but now is the time to concentrate," or "Yeah, this is a pressure-packed moment, so hang on for the ride." It's natural to feel nervous, and even professional and recreational players admit to having nerves. The champions are the ones who accept their nerves and continue playing instead of suppressing them and freezing up.

4. Anchors.

Before a game, create and choose an anchor that makes you feel calm. It could be a song, the feeling of relaxing at the beach, or the emotions you feel when you're with a loved one. When things get rough during the game, focus on recalling the sounds, sights, and feelings associated with that anchor. By allowing yourself this mental break, you can return to the game with a fresh outlook.

5. Cue cards.

Before a game, prepare a cue card with a few pertinent words, phrases, or quotes that may help you relax. Write statements on the card such as "Focus on what you can control," "I don't have to be perfect," or simply "Breathe." Then, attach the cue card to your towel and refer to the ideas on it between games for inspiration and a feeling of calm.

6. Breathing.

Bring your attention to your breath— the body and the breath are always in the present moment. By simply noticing your breath's natural rhythm, whether it's the sound or the feel of it, you can bring yourself into the present and calm yourself down. Sometimes, in the heat of the moment, noticing your breath can be too

tricky or passive for some players, causing them to become impatient. If this happens to you, remember to breathe in relaxation and breathe out stress. Say or think the words as you do this. Another breathing exercise is to inhale to the count of three and exhale to the count of four. You might even discover your own breathing rhythm when you are playing.

7. Eye-of-the-hurricane focus.

To use the eye-of-the-hurricane focus, simply bring your attention to an object and focus on it. This narrowing of your focus will help you eliminate outside distractions. You may want to focus on the sound of the ball off your paddle or even the sweat dripping from your brow. Once you are focused on your object of choice, you can then begin to expand your focus and take in everything around you. You will find this narrow-to-wide focusing to be very calming.

Regaining focus on what you can control can be challenging. However, learning to adapt to the situation and conditions of the day will empower you, and this is key to playing your best. Remember, the above tools can help you slow down, relax, and move beyond adverse situations.

You Cannot Be Serious!

Tools to Help You Regain Your Focus

The idea behind concentration is not necessarily to focus 100% of the time, but to know when you have lost your focus and regain it. Try the exercises below for five minutes each.

NO DISTRACTION EXERCISE:

Step #1: With your eyes closed, notice your breath as you inhale and exhale.

Step #2: As you inhale, visualize the number 1; as you exhale, silently say the number 1. Repeat this process.

Step #3: If you get distracted or lose focus of the number 1, gently move on to the number 2 and visualize the number 2.

What number did you reach? _____

What did you do when you lost your concentration? _____

_____

DISTRACTION EXERCISE:

Now, let's incorporate distractions. Turn on the TV, or have a friend try to distract you. Either way, close your eyes and follow the no-distraction protocol. Expect to lose your focus many more times.

What number did you reach? _____

_____

How was this different? _____

_____

_____

_____

Is it bad that you're losing your focus? _____

_____

The answer is no: What is important is understanding that you *will* lose your focus. What's key is bringing your focus back to what's important and what you can control at that time. It's impossible to focus 100% of the time. The top pros know how to relax and then focus at key times.

When you lose your focus, what are two things you can do to regain it?

1. _____

2. _____

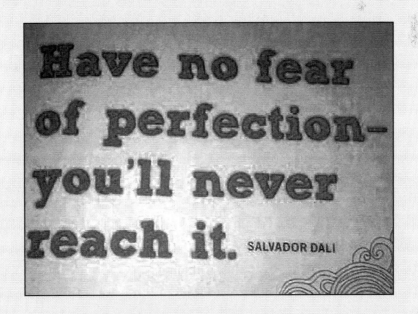

Workout 22
Mental Principles

- If it were easy, everybody would be doing it.
- An opponent is most dangerous when they have nothing to lose.
- Closing out a match is hard. Expect that!

Match Point... Relax!
Five Steps to Closing Out a Match

The Rose

When we plant a rose in the earth,
We notice that it is small but we do not criticize it. As rootless and stemless, We treat it as a seed, Giving it the water and nourishment
Required of a seed. When it first shoots up
Out of the earth, we don't condemn it
As immature and underdeveloped;
Nor do we criticize the buds for not being open When they appear. We stand in wonder
At the process taking place and give the plant
The care it needs at each stage of its development.
The rose is a rose from the time it is a seed
To the time it dies. Within it, at all times
It contains its full potential. It seems to be
Constantly in the process of change; yet at each state, at each moment It's perfectly alright, perfectly okay,

Just as it is.

— **W. Timothy Galwey**, *The Inner Game of Tennis*

Match Point...Relax!

How many times have you found yourself in a match where you were just a few points or games away from winning? Maybe the score was 11-9, 8-5, and you began to think, 'Oh my gosh, this is great. I am going to win!' or 'Only three more points and I have the victory!' or even 'My friends are going to think I am better than him or her.' In another situation, you might be even closer to the finish line. Perhaps you are leading 11-9, 10-8 and serving for the final point, when you begin to think, 'Just one more point!

All recreational, tournament, and professional players have had these thoughts. The question is, how many of them have succumbed to such thoughts and gone on to lose the match? The answer is: too many! While it is true that many professionals and top-ranked players may lose their focus during critical times in a match, the truly mentally tough competitors become aware when this happens and are able to change and regain their focus immediately.

Paradoxically, losing focus is not horrible. In fact, it is a natural occurrence. The key is to be aware that you have lost your focus and then change it to bring yourself back to the present moment. The problem is that when it happens, you may swear that you are concentrating and you probably are, but just on the wrong thing! Focusing on future events immediately removes you from the present moment and takes you to a place where you have no control. Moreover, as your thoughts drift into the future, you lose touch with what is really important, such as relying on your instincts, trusting your game, and playing without thinking, which are the things that brought you to this point—the point where you can compete at your best.

When you lose focus, you usually begin to get tight physiologically. The blood flow gets diverted away from your hands and feet toward your deeper muscle groups, and your breathing becomes labored instead of deep and rhythmic. Next comes a loss of feel for your strokes. You are no longer focused on what you can control but instead worrying about your opponent, what others are going to say, and how you will explain away the loss. All of these physiological responses, combined with future-oriented thinking, cause your game to spiral farther out of control, particularly as you lose the next point, gasp for breath, grip the racket tighter, and try to find that elusive feel you had earlier.

So what can a player do? No doubt, this is a difficult situation. But by employing the following five mental-toughness strategies, especially when you find yourself trying to close out a game or match, you can give yourself the opportunity to get back on track and turn things around.

1. Become aware.

The first step to combating a loss of focus is to become aware that you have indeed lost it. When we talk about "concentration" in the sports arena, we are referring to the ability to focus on what is important and to let go of everything else. All players lose their focus at times; it is inevitable. The truly mentally tough players understand this. They do not beat themselves up when it happens, and they immediately bring their focus back to what they can control.

2. Refocus on the present.

This step is imperative, but how can you achieve it? First off, know that it takes a lot of courage and discipline to mentally refocus. However, what's the alternative? A free-fall! To refocus, shift your attention to your breath. Your breath is always in the present moment: simply listen to its rhythm, sound, and feel as it enters and leaves your body. Alternatively, visualize yourself inhaling relaxation and exhaling stress, slowly letting go of the tension with each breath. Another exercise for present-moment awareness is to inhale through your nose to the count of three (if possible) and exhale through your mouth to the count of four, or create your own pattern. These relaxation techniques will help you stay calm, relaxed, and mentally present during the most challenging moments of a match.

3. Change your focus.

Athletes tend to lose focus when they think about the future, such as what might happen on the next point. The key here is to recognize this loss of focus and bring yourself back to the current point. Ask yourself, "What's important right now?" This phrase will help you stay in the present moment.

4. Let go of winning and expectations.

Remember, you cannot control whether you win or lose, or whether you hit a winner—your opponent has a say in that. Likewise, you cannot control the expectations others have of you. Paradoxically, the harder you try to close out the match point and win, the more physically tight you will become. Just play each point to the best of your ability; if you do this, you will put yourself in the best position to win. If you don't win, you can walk away feeling positive about your effort.

5. Trust the process.

Bring your attention to what you have to do to win the crucial point, which might include staying relaxed, returning the ball deep, or serving into your opponent's backhand. Ask yourself what it would feel like to hit a great serve. Your body knows; now is the time to trust it. Then ask yourself what it would feel like to play this point relaxed, and instinctively you will feel a release. In The Inner Game of Tennis, W. Timothy Gallwey talks about letting your body play the way it knows how to without interference from your (thinking) brain.

Using the strategies above will help you win the next point, game, or match. This is because they help you to begin the point in a calm and relaxed place. Remember, match point…relax!…now you know how!

Match Point...Relax!

Try Softer, Not Harder

One of the biggest mental traps that athletes fall into is **"trying too hard."** **Fueled by frustration** or making the contest too important, trying too hard is usually a game of diminishing returns: The harder you try, the worse you'll do!

This is because **you put pressure on yourself**, rush yourself, and your **muscles tighten up**.

Peak performance always comes from being in a **state of relaxed awareness**, a place of letting go, where the actions happen without much conscious effort or thought.

When you become aware of **yourself trying too hard**, pressing, or rushing...**Shift your focus** of concentration away from the outcome or its importance to the present task at hand.

Remember you want to **relax and try "softer," not harder**.

What does the passage above make you aware of? _____

_____

How does this apply to your game? _____

_____

In order to try softer, not harder, what are three things you could do?

1. _____

2. _____

3. _____

Workout 23
Mental Principles

- Let go, relax, the point will still be there.
- Use the towel to refresh and refocus.
- During time outs and game changes use your towel. It provides a moment to refresh and recharge.

The Towel is Your Friend
How to Stay Calm Before Each Game

Just Let Go!

Can you remember a time you wanted to do something but were fearful, hesitant, or anxious to "just let go" and "go for it?"

Maybe it was a particular shot you wanted to hit, a strategic decision that might have changed the course of a game, or changing your focus from what you can control away from what you couldn't…

So imagine this…life is the ocean and you're a surfer just learning to surf. At first, you're fearful, hesitant, and anxious to get into the water.

At a certain point you realize if you want to surf you must let go and be willing to trust the ocean and yourself. Trusting to go with the flow…

The paradoxical situation is that once you go with the flow it usually feels easier; the water carries you. Once you become comfortable with the ocean and your balance, you can begin to look ahead, decide which waves to ride, and which course would be best. Steering away from trouble, rocks and other surfers. Simply choosing the best line while still going with the flow.

This story illustrates how we can be with our experience in the here and now, flowing with what is, while at the same time directing ourselves towards our goals with purpose, passion, and perseverance.

—**Rob Polishook**, MA CPC, Mental Training Coach

The Towel is Your Friend

How many times have you seen a player step off the line to take a breath? Or, during a break between games or a time-out, take a moment to towel off? Do you bring your towel to the court when you play a match? In tight situations, do you make time to catch your breath? And during game breaks or timeouts, do you walk over to your towel to give yourself a momentary break from the action?

I suggest taking the time to retrieve your towel whenever possible, as it can become your best friend on the court. In addition to wiping off perspiration from your face and arms, your towel can offer much more than you may realize! It's a built-in break, providing separation from the pressure of the match. Although not like going to your favorite ice cream shop or the beach, it can give you the necessary time to relax, bring your heart rate down, slow your breathing, and, most importantly, decompress and center yourself for the next game. Bring a towel that feels good on your body, which can also help relax your nervous system. Retrieving your towel as a ritual creates familiarity, keeping you comfortable on the court and helping you stay in the present.

As a player, you cannot directly control future points since you cannot control your opponent. However, you can determine whether you approach the line to serve or return serve on your own terms, while remaining focused and centered. Remember to take a deep breath and use your towel whenever you have the chance.

The Towel is Your Friend

Have you noticed that most professional tennis and pickleball players towel off whenever the opportunity presents itself? It's not just because they sweat more than non-pros. They know something that many recreational players may not: taking a moment to towel off can help you regain and stay focused and composed on the court. By wiping off the sweat and regrouping, you can shake off any mistakes from the previous game and approach the next one with a clear mind. So, whether you're a beginner or a seasoned player, consider adopting the habit of toweling off to help you stay at the top of your game.

The towel is your friend. It can help you:

- Slow things down
- Catch your breath
- Relax and get centered
- Compose yourself
- Let go of the previous game
- Wipe sweat off your head and hands!

Have you considered attaching an index card to the corner of your towel? On the card, you could include a quote or phrase that motivates you, or a few things that you want to remember during the match. These should be non-technical items that offer insight, relaxation, and motivation. They should also be customized to the specific match, opponent, and circumstance.

As an example, on my index card, I usually write things like:

By glancing at the card between games and timeouts, I am reminded of my intentions and can stay mentally focused throughout the match. Consider creating your own index card to help you stay motivated and centered during your matches.

Mental Reminders

- Trust your instincts
- Stay aggressive
- Breathe and stay calm
- Have fun and enjoy the game
- Focus on what you can control
- The next shot is the most important shot
- Compete like a tiger

Workout 24
Mental Principles

- Play to WIN (what's important now).
- Your opponent is your partner, not your enemy.
- Play within yourself, not without!

Competing In the Trenches
One Part Skill, Three Parts Will

ON COURT DRILL
Chaos

Purpose: Improve the ability to handle high-pressure shots, especially in situations with limited time for setup.

Drill:
- One player stands right up to the net, even touching it.
- The other player positions themselves in the transition zone.
- The player at the net feeds the ball to the other player at different heights (low, high).
- The goal of the transition zone player is to return the ball and neutralize the continuous barrage of shots.
- The player at the net is allowed to lean over and hit balls that don't cross the net, contributing to the chaotic rally.
- This "chaos" practice takes place using half the court, with shots directed either down the line or cross court.

Progressions: The difficulty of the feeds and subsequent shots can be increased based on the challenge and skill level of the players.

Mental Intention: The player in the transition zone should effectively field and return challenging shots. Shots may be directed at their feet and driven forcefully at them. Both players must maintain composure and stay relaxed during the drill. The emphasis is on perseverance, staying calm under pressure, and responding to each shot individually. The player in the transition zone is on the defense, and their goal is to keep the point going for one more shot.

Competing In the Trenches

It's 95 degrees, and the sun is beating down with no cloud cover in sight as I step onto the pickleball court. The air is thick and moist, and the court surface is hot enough to fry an egg! The rubber on my soles is burning, and my legs feel like live wires. As I look for cover, I see a sliver of shade behind the baseline in the corner by the fence. I've been out here for 3 hours and 20 minutes and have advanced to the quarterfinals of this tournament. The match has just begun. I remember what my coach said: 'Tournaments are three parts will and one part skill.' At this point, I know it's all about how I compete.

I reflect back and remember the hours of drilling I put in, stretching, lifting weights, and conditioning myself for these moments. I also think of all the mental training I have practiced. Ugh, but I'm tired. I wonder if I even have enough left. It's decision time. Either I push through and compete or give in and fold. Another thought crosses my mind…why am I doing this in the first place? Yet I have made it my motto to compete to the fullest each and every point of each and every game. I remind myself to bring my attention to my breath—it's so simple, but always seems to calm me and bring me into the present.

Up to this point, the matches have been a battle—the momentum has been like waves in the ocean, one after another, relentlessly crashing over each other. I still can't believe how we have stayed so resilient and worked through any adversity we have faced. Okay, that's in the past. It's game time! Every point is important. I remember my coach saying, 'The key to ideal competing is adapting and adjusting to what is currently happening.' Yes, we won 11-9, 11-7. On to the semifinals!

I know a change in strategy is essential to beat the next team. Their soft game is precise. It's time to mix it up, pick our targets while staying patient. I need to really pick the right shots to speed up on; in fact, just think one more shot when dinking. 'The ability to be aware of what is going on in a match and be willing to change strategy when necessary is what separates the top 1% of competitors from the other 99%.'"

This match, we are playing some guy named McNasty! He's a West Coast guy and a former tennis player with soft hands. My mental training coach says, 'There are many things that you can't control, such as who you play, how your opponent plays or acts. You cannot control the sun that has just begun to peek out from behind the clouds. You cannot directly control the result of this match—you can only control yourself, the shots you choose, and how you handle your emotions.'".

Overall, I feel solid, trying to push through all the distractions. Is this what some top players feel like in big matches? I remind myself to stay focused on what I can control in my game. My job is to get myself in a position where I can enter the next point in a calm, centered place. I use my breath to help me stay in the present and relax.

Ugh, we lost the first game 11-7. I need to change my strategy for the return points. It's time to hit deeper and float balls to his backhand side. If I can throw my opponent off his rhythm, maybe I can get him off his game? My ego tells me to keep pounding the ball, to try to overpower him, but I know I have to push this aside. I need to focus on my backhand, play softer shots, and get to the kitchen. I cannot worry about what other people think about my game, which is just another uncontrollable factor. I must do what I think is best to win and put aside any other concerns.

Ahhh, we lost the second game and I am now out of the tournament. This match was disappointing but certainly something to learn from. As I reflect back on the tournament, I realize that it wasn't entirely about skill but about competing in the moment. I had to adapt and adjust to the game's momentum, focus on what I could control, and let go of what I could not. I had to battle without expectations, be willing to put my ego aside, and through it all, I had to stay alert. These are the skills necessary to compete at your highest level.

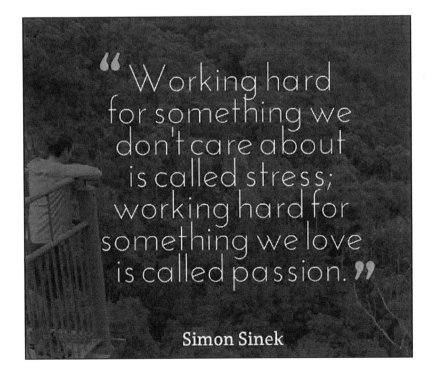

"Working hard for something we don't care about is called stress; working hard for something we love is called passion."

Simon Sinek

Competing In the Trenches

Pre-Round Intangibles Scale

Through this exercise, you can rate, become aware of, and better understand key intangible factors prior to a match against a rival. Rate yourself and your opponent on each of these measurements using a scale of 0 to 10, where 0 means not at all and 10 means very much. If you are unable to rate your opponent, complete the exercise only by rating yourself.

Opponent: _____

Tournament: _____

Date: _____

Confidence	Myself	Field
Momentum coming into the match		
Experience factor		
Physical readiness		
Mental readiness		
Hunger factor		
Ability to focus on controllables		
Ability to manage uncomfortable situations		
Ability to make opponent uncomfortable		
Ability to stay emotionally balanced, and refocus		
Awareness		
Ability to stay the course (resilience, tenacity)		
Ability to bounce back from adversity/obstacles/setbacks (perseverance)		

Confidence	Myself	Field
Ability to adapt/adjust, switch plans (flexibility)		
Ability to make high-percentage choices		
Ability to play within self, take what the course is giving you (patience)		

What does analyzing the Intangibles Scale make you aware of? _____

_____

_____

_____

What are you aware of in relation to your opponent? _____

_____

_____

_____

From the above, what are three things that would help you as you prepare for your round?

1. _____

2. _____

3. _____

Workout 25
Mental Principles

- Sometimes it's about three parts will and one part skill.

- Pickleball is like a roller coaster ride, with many ups and downs. Just hold on tight!

- It's not how you start, but how you finish.

Riding the Waves
Using Momentum to Win in Competition

ON COURT DRILL
Riding the Wave

Purpose: This simulation drill is designed to replicate the inevitable momentum shifts that occur in a match.

Drill:
- Two players engage in a game of their choice, playing to 11 points.
- Players can select a dink game at the kitchen, skinny singles, or any preferred game for practice.
- One player has the opportunity to initiate a "momentum shift" in the score if they are behind.
- For instance, if the score is 4 points to 7, the trailing player can shift the score to their advantage, making it 7 points to 4.
- The game then continues and is played until one player reaches 11 points.

Progressions:
- This game can be played with two or four players, adapting to any game they choose. Be creative in your selections.
- Additionally, players can opt to incorporate more than one momentum shift, although I recommend using an odd number of shifts.

Mental Intention: The mental intention for the player who was ahead but due to the momentum shift is now losing is to experience a sudden loss of points. This simulates scenarios where unforced errors or great shots by their opponent lead to a change in score. However, the player should maintain their resiliency, not fold under pressure, and continue playing. Conversely, for the player who was behind and is now ahead due to the momentum shift, the intention is to build upon this sudden positive change in momentum.

Riding the Waves

A surfer sits in the open ocean, enjoying the tranquility of the calm waters while staying in control on his surfboard. However, he ventures out in search of the big wave that will satisfy his craving for competition and push him to his limits. The surfer embraces the challenge and looks forward to the biggest wave that may come his way. Riding the wave will test his physical abilities and mental game, leaving him wondering if he can come out unscathed. If he can stay on the board and ride the wave out, he will be ready for whatever comes next. But if he spirals out of control and is thrashed under the water, he will have no ability to take advantage of calm seas or handle a new wave.

There are parallels between this anecdote and pickleball competition. Just as a surfer begins a session in control, a pickleball player may start a match confidently making shots and winning points. But like a wave in the ocean, a shift in momentum is bound to occur in a match. This natural evolution is beyond anyone's control, and consistency plays a small role in both nature and sports. The best strategy is to continue battling and ride out the momentum shift.

A surfer spots a wave approaching in the distance, just as a pickleball player senses a change in momentum before it shows on the scoreboard. This shift can manifest as unforced errors or an opponent's boost in the game. External factors like poor line calls or fan conduct can also cause a momentum swing. However, players can mentally prepare for these situations by staying aware and hunkering down. Sometimes, the waves are sudden, and the player must hang on and grind it out to stay afloat.

Metaphorically, the wave represents a shift in momentum that's often beyond the player's control. It can be caused by a great shot from the opponent or a lucky bounce. Rather than viewing it as an obstacle, it should be seen as an opportunity to test one's ability to stay focused, adapt, and adjust one's game. It's a chance to push oneself both mentally and physically towards success.

To achieve success, a player must proactively ride out the wave and stay afloat by grinding and staying focused. Players have demonstrated this countless times by side out points. Once the wave passes, the calm resumes. The crucial question is whether the player has managed to stay on the board or has been thrown off by the wave. If the player is still on the board, they can prepare to battle once the momentum shifts in their favor. However, if the player dwells on past points, feels sorry for themselves, or is despondent about the negative turn of events, they may be unaware that the wave has passed. In such cases, the player will continue to spiral out of control and miss out on the opportunity to take advantage of the newfound calm after the storm.

A player must recognize that momentum shifts are unavoidable in competition; it is just part of the rhythm of a game or match. Just as waves in the ocean ebb and flow, the course of a match constantly changes as well. This is a natural phenomenon and the reason why we find pickleball so entertaining. Waves, momentum shifts, and adversity in a match should be seen as a challenge, something to be embraced. Perhaps Billie Jean King said it best when she said her infamous line, "Pressure is a privilege."

In the end, riding the big wave is the ultimate thrill. A surfer may struggle with the wave but still stay on the board and ride it out, or they may completely fall off the board and capsize. When a surfer stays calm under pressure, they can persevere no matter how big or how many waves come their way. Once the surfer knows they can handle the waves, they can embrace even bigger waves and hope for even bigger challenges. Only by challenging oneself and confronting increasingly bigger obstacles can one improve. No one is saying that the waves will be easy to ride out. The objective is to battle it and stay afloat. Only by embracing the challenge of a big wave and testing one's limits can true potential be uncovered. Remember, nothing great is ever achieved without overcoming adversity.

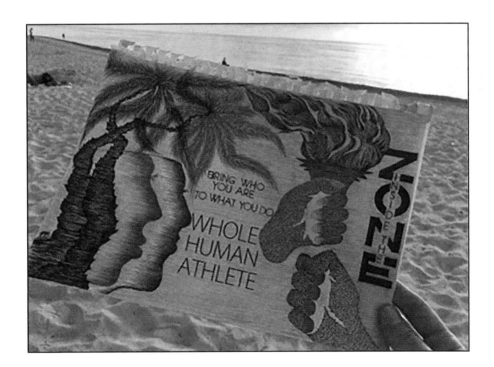

Riding the Waves

Hello–Goodbye Exercise

Imagine you are playing a game, whether it be pickleball, tennis, or another sport. Each point presents an opportunity to embrace something new, like saying hello to the nervousness of people watching, and to let go of something that is holding you back, like saying goodbye to the fear of being judged. By taking advantage of these opportunities, you can improve your mental game and perform at your best.

Now, as you imagine playing the game, continue to fill in the blanks.

FIRST ROUND

Example: Hello: *Nervousness of people watching*   Goodbye: *Fear of being judged*

Shot 1: Hello: _____   Goodbye: _____

Shot 2: Hello: _____   Goodbye: _____

Shot 3: Hello: _____   Goodbye: _____

Shot 4: Hello: _____   Goodbye: _____

Shot 5: Hello: _____   Goodbye: _____

Shot 6: Hello: _____   Goodbye: _____

Shot 7: Hello: _____   Goodbye: _____

Shot 8: Hello: _____   Goodbye: _____

Shot 9: Hello: _____   Goodbye: _____

Shot 9: Hello: _____   Goodbye: _____

Shot 10: Hello: _____   Goodbye: _____

Shot 11: Hello: _____   Goodbye: _____

Workout 26
Mental Principles

- Remember your training; trust your instincts.
- Overthinking leads to paralysis.
- Listen carefully—your body knows what to do.

Get Outta Your Mind
It's the Only Way to Compete!

Try Softer, Not Harder

One of the most significant mental traps that athletes fall into is "trying too hard." Driven by frustration or attaching too much significance to the competition, trying too hard often results in diminishing returns. The harder you try, the more likely your performance will suffer. This happens because you create self-imposed pressure, rush yourself, and tense up your muscles.

Peak performance emerges from a state of relaxed awareness, where you let go of the need to force things. It's a place where actions flow without excessive conscious effort or overthinking.

When you recognize yourself trying too hard, pushing too much, or rushing, shift your focus away from the outcome or its importance. Instead, redirect your attention to the present task at hand. Remember, your aim is to relax and try "softer," not harder.

—**Rob Polishook**, author

Get Outta Your Mind

We have all heard people say, 'She played out of her mind!' referring to someone who played exceptionally well beyond expectations. As an athlete, have you ever performed out of your mind? Perhaps you couldn't miss a third shot drop or your hands were unusually solid? Maybe there is more to this 'out of your mind' concept than meets the eye. Ultimately, the idea is a metaphor for playing within yourself, where everything is effortless, little thought occurs, and optimal performance just happens. In this workout, I will discuss how getting 'out of your mind' literally is the best way to reach optimal peak performance in competitive sports.

When a pickleball player plays 'in their mind,' they are not playing from instinct. They are usually over-analyzing, and their thoughts are cluttered and disorganized. These thoughts interfere with their ability to play well. Furthermore, these thoughts tend to focus on the past and the future, tied to expectations, ego, excitement, and fears. Essentially, these thoughts weigh them down, and athletes describe it as playing with an imaginary weight around their waist. It can make it difficult to run, jump, hit, and concentrate while their mind is over-thinking every move.

We all know what happens when this kind of mentality creeps in—the dreaded spiral where a player loses control!

Physically and mentally, it looks like this: an initial loss of focus, fear about what might be or what is occurring, tightened muscles, heavy breathing, and loss of feeling. Then, poor play follows, usually ending in disappointment and defeat. The only way to optimize performance is to play in the moment (present) and respond to situations with calm awareness, as opposed to reacting out of ego, fear, and anxiety. I call this the 'eye of the hurricane,' where you remain calm on the inside yet aware and active on the outside.

The key to staying in the moment is within all of us—the secret lies in our bodies. Our body is always in the present moment. When an athlete becomes aware of his or her body, such as the rhythm when they swing a paddle, they simplify things and enter a place of curiosity where they are simply noticing their present actions. This moves them away from distracting ego, fear, and anxiety-driven thoughts. In fact, all of the 'what-if,' 'shoulda,' or 'coulda' thoughts are no longer in the way because the focus is on observation rather than judgment. Essentially, by getting 'out of your mind,' you get 'out of your way' and simply allow the strokes you have practiced and your performance to happen or flow in the present. If an adjustment is necessary, it can then be made without judgment.

How can a player shift their focus 'out of their mind' (thoughts, past, future, and judgments) and into their body (present)? It starts with keen awareness. When they become aware of being submerged in overthinking, fear, or that recognizable negative spiral, the idea is to simplify things and shift attention to something in the present. For example, the athlete may focus on their breathing or a place in the body where they feel calm and centered. This refocus 'out of your mind' and into your body serves as a reconnection to the present—a place of calm and observation. From this place, the athlete can play by observing and noticing instead of judging their technique or performance."

Ultimately, at the start of the game, the athlete has the necessary skills to compete at their personal highest level. The competition is not the time to analyze technique but rather an opportunity to simply play by getting "out of your mind" and allowing the body to do what it has been trained to do. It is easy for the mind to wander towards the end result, getting caught up in expectations, questioning whether others are judging your performance, or thinking about missed opportunities from previous exchanges. However, the aforementioned tools can help the player keep their attention out of their mind and in the present, enabling them to respond to the moment.

Athletes love those times when they feel immersed in the competition, exerting great effort for sustained periods of time, and ultimately playing inside the zone. So, in the next competition, shift your focus "outta your mind," away from fears or judgments, and "into the zone," focusing on your breath and body, and begin the path to unlocking your potential.

> Today you are You,
> that is truer than true.
> There is no one alive
> Who is Youer than you.
>
> —Dr. Seuss

Get Outta Your Mind

The Frog and the Centipede

A frog was sitting on a patch of grass by his pond one sunny morning when a large centipede passed by.

The frog watched this creature with fascination, then said, "Excuse me, can I ask you a question?"

"Why, yes, of course," replied the centipede, pausing in his stride.

"I am amazed at the way you can proceed so harmoniously with your one hundred legs," said the frog. "Can you explain to me how you manage to keep them in order?"

The centipede reflected for a moment. "You know, I have never really thought about it," he said. "Let me see if I can demonstrate it for you."

And he started to walk, thinking about which leg should follow another. Immediately, he fell down and had great difficulty getting up again.

"You are dangerous!" he said to the frog angrily. "Never again ask such questions!"

After reading this poem, what does it make you aware of? _____

_____

How does this relate to your pickleball game? _____

_____

List three ways this insight can help your game:

1. _____

2. _____

3. _____

Pickle and the Pros

PICKLEBALL
INSIDE THE
ZONE

Section 4
POST-MATCH WORKOUTS

Post-Round Workouts

It's All Practice

Martial artists understand that competition brings with it a separate set of challenges, therefore whether they win or lose, They see it as practice and part of the journey.

Martial artists understand success is reached along the journey, not at the destination. They see the competition as something to learn and grow from. Further obstacles, failures and successes are to be expected and necessary experiences in striving for a goal.

What would happen if you approached games and tournaments the same way martial articles approach competition?

—**Rob Polishook**, *author*

Workout 27
Mental Principles

- You only truly lose when you give up.
- Losing provides an opportunity for a fresh start.
- Failure serves as valuable feedback and is an integral part of the process.

Losing Stinks!
Five ways to dealing with a tough loss

Whole Human Athlete Rap

You're a whole human athlete, a person too
There are no limits on what you can do
Like the rising sun, beautiful and free
The powers inside, the challenge is to be.

Bring your talent, bring your skills
And all the stuff you do in drills
But don't forget who you are
You are a pickleball star!

Losing Stinks!

Imagine this: You're playing on the challenge court, grinding it out on the hard courts under the scorching sun. The first game ends in a hard-fought win of 11-8. However, in the tightly contested second game, you narrowly lose 10-12, even after holding two match points! Now, you find yourself in the third game, and the score is 9-10. Suddenly, your opponent's shot hits the net, trickles over, and you hear an echoing thought in your head: "game, match." It's yet another disappointing loss, but this time, it cuts even deeper. The pain intensifies as you had two match points in the second game and multiple opportunities to seal victory in the third. Slowly, you approach the net, exchanging paddle taps with your partner and opponents. Your hand feels limp, your body drained of energy as if a vacuum cleaner sucked it away. Your legs tremble, and your eyes remain glazed over. It's simply unfathomable what has just unfolded before your eyes.

So, what's a player supposed to do? How can you overcome this overwhelming disappointment? Your friends, who are also avid players, nonchalantly tell you it's no big deal, to just move on. They assure you that you'll perform better next time. Don't you hate that phrase? However, despite being drenched in sweat and feeling partially paralyzed, you manage to hear their words, although you can barely respond. It's as if you're struck with a lockjaw, unable to utter a single word. Inside your mind, you're incessantly replaying the points that you believe you should have won, desperately clutching onto those missed opportunities.

So, let me reiterate…what is a player supposed to do? How do you cope with the disappointment? How do you bounce back from a painful defeat? First and foremost, let's acknowledge the undeniable truth: It's neither easy nor pleasant! Nevertheless, there comes a point when the pain begins to subside, be it within a few hours or a day. At this juncture, it becomes crucial to adopt a different perspective on the match. How do you go about picking up the shattered pieces? What steps must you take to improve next time? How will you seize opportunities and consistently position yourself to overcome obstacles?

The following five steps are designed to assist you, the disheartened player, in experiencing and overcoming a disappointing performance. Equally valuable, this list serves as an excellent resource for parents, coaches, and friends who seek to support the player throughout the stages of disappointment, release, and recovery.

1. The right to feel disappointed.

You have earned the right to feel disappointed. Let's be honest: after giving it your all, pouring your heart into the competition, it's nearly impossible to put on a smile and simply forget about things after a closely fought loss. Allow yourself some time. It's perfectly okay to feel disappointed. In fact, it's expected. Why wouldn't you be? You deeply care, you've put in countless hours of practice, you're a warrior, and you fought like one! Disappointment is a natural emotion—it even hurts, and that's completely fine. It's not something that requires an immediate fix. Time is usually the healer. Disappointment can be likened to mourning a loss. Grant yourself the space to decompress, acknowledge your emotions, and find inner calm. Paradoxically, by allowing yourself to embrace the disappointment, you also open doors to release and resolve the painful feelings. One of the factors that makes victory so incredibly sweet and drives our motivation is the profound understanding and experience of disappointment.

2. One step closer.

Believe it or not, you have actually taken one step closer towards your goals! Take inspiration from the legendary Babe Ruth, who used to say, "Every time I strike out, I'm one step closer to hitting a home run!" Babe would learn from each time he stepped up to the plate, adjusting his strategies accordingly. You can do the same. It may seem like you're going nowhere or even regressing, but keep persevering and learning. Perhaps the competition has become tougher, or the matchup is less favorable. Remember the saying: "It's always darkest before dawn." In other words, the sun rises after the darkest hour! That slump you're experiencing might be a significant learning curve that simply needs to be endured, much like riding out a wave. Just beyond that wave lies smooth sailing. Hold on tight…

3. Failure offers valuable feedback.

If you listen, you become aware. Failures, setbacks, and obstacles can often catch us off guard, but it's the true champion who can readjust and extract valuable feedback. Feedback should be approached without judgment, seen as an opportunity for learning, enabling you to make necessary changes and adapt for the future. Consider this: Has there ever been a great champion, whether an individual or a team, who didn't learn from failures, setbacks, and obstacles? All exceptional champions understand the reasons behind their competition and utilize their "Big Why" to regain their focus. How long were fans critical of Federer during his early days? They claimed he was just hype. However, Federer was silently proving himself, taking on opponents, and continuously learning from each experience along the way.

4. Reframe it!

After you have decompressed, take a moment to ask yourself some fundamental questions. How can you view this loss or situation from a different perspective? Is there a way to find something positive in it? What valuable lessons can be learned, despite the defeat? And let's not forget: Give yourself credit for having the courage to show up and put yourself on the line. Consider how few others are competing with the same level of heart and determination as you.

5. Focus on the process, not the outcome.
Undoubtedly, this is one of the most crucial points, encompassing the essence of all other points. Although you may have experienced a loss in this particular performance, it represents another significant stride toward your ultimate goal. The match has granted you invaluable experience and exposed you to the pressure of real-time competition. This exposure is immensely precious and cannot be replicated in practice alone. Always bear in mind that every great champion has had to pay their dues along the journey.

Gumbo loves Papa... win or lose!

Losing Stinks!

It's not how hard you can hit that matters, it's how hard you can get hit, and keep bouncing back—that's what life (sports) is about.

— **Sylvester Stallone**, *Rocky*

First and foremost, let's acknowledge that it is indeed painful to experience defeat, particularly when you have invested yourself fully and given your best effort in that specific situation and moment. Secondly, let's recognize that bouncing back from a painful loss is undoubtedly challenging, but it is within your capability to overcome it!

What was a time you experienced a difficult loss? Describe it: _____

_____

_____

_____

What are three things you learned from the loss?

1. _____

2. _____

3. _____

How can you use these lessons in future matches? _____

_____

_____

If you did, what would happen? _____

_____

Workout 28
Mental Principles

- Setbacks and obstacles serve as valuable feedback for growth and improvement.

- Success is not measured by how hard you can hit, but by how hard you can be hit and still bounce back.

- Success is not determined by whether you make mistakes, but rather by how you rebound from them.

Mistakes, Setbacks and Failure
The Only Way to Win

Heart of a Champion

H   Humility

E   Equanimity

A   Awareness

R   Respect

T   Truth

Mistakes, Setbacks and Failure

Nobody enjoys making mistakes during practice, encountering setbacks and obstacles in games, or experiencing failure and defeat in tournaments. It's painful, disappointing, frustrating, and can sometimes feel like starting over from the beginning. However, there is a secret—a secret that top players understand but many recreational players and aspiring juniors fail to grasp. This secret lies in the understanding that mistakes, setbacks, obstacles, and failure are unavoidable. Furthermore, it's how a player learns from and adapts to these challenging experiences that ultimately determines whether they fulfill their potential.

Indeed, top players experience disappointment due to mistakes, setbacks, obstacles, and losing— in fact, they despise them more than anyone else. However, they also recognize that these challenges are an inevitable part of their journey. They refuse to let setbacks sidetrack them as they relentlessly pursue their ultimate goal: continuous improvement and long-term success.

Allow me to share an example of a tennis player who was notorious for being a hothead during his junior years. Starting his professional career ranked #803, in his first year, he achieved two wins and suffered three losses. The following year, he faced first-round exits in every outdoor tournament he participated in, went 0-2 in the Davis Cup, failed to reach the main draw in two Grand Slam tournaments, and concluded the season with 12 wins and 14 losses. In his third year, he experienced first-round defeats in 21 out of 38 ATP tournaments, concluding the year with 30 wins and 27 losses. After presenting this background, I once posed a question to a group of juniors: "What would you do if you were this player?" Most of them raised their hands and expressed their intention to quit and pursue another profession. Thankfully, Roger Federer had different plans!

This reminds me of a phrase I frequently use: "Failure is feedback." This expression highlights the concept that failure serves as a valuable opportunity for athletes. It allows them to gather feedback from negative experiences and make necessary adjustments and improvements to their game. These adaptations swiftly guide them back on the right track towards their goals. However, if a player lacks awareness of their own weaknesses, they will persist in repeating the same actions and making the same mistakes, leading to a downward spiral.

Another renowned phrase is "Failure is breakfast for champions." This phrase emphasizes the importance of failure in the learning process of athletes. To acquire better methods, athletes must experience failure repeatedly. They need to take risks, engage in experimentation, and foster curiosity. While such experimentation may bring about failures, it also opens the door to success. Consider the example of a skier or a surfer: If they never fall, it's likely that the slopes or waves aren't challenging enough. Skiers and surfers, in fact, constantly seek the next exhilarating challenge. They are never content with repeating the same run; instead, they strive for steeper hills or more massive waves.

You don't have to like failure; in fact, you can even hate it! However, it's crucial to recognize that failure is a necessary part of the journey toward success. It's understandable to feel disappointed and even angry after a setback. Nevertheless, this state of mind doesn't have to be permanent. By developing heightened awareness of what went wrong, you can begin working through the factors that may have contributed to the outcome. Just because you played poorly today doesn't mean you will perform poorly every day. Your future results are not predetermined. Losing a match doesn't define you as a loser; it simply means you lost on that particular day. Tomorrow brings a fresh start with a new opponent. Moreover, it's essential to understand that your primary opponent is yourself, and the competition exists to help you assess your progress and enhance your skills. Lastly, recognizing that you are a work in progress and not a fixed entity paves the way for improvement, change, and the possibility of achieving different results.

The key point here is that winning is a process riddled with setbacks, mistakes, obstacles, and failures. When approached correctly, athletes will view these setbacks as temporary. They can learn from them and ultimately progress toward their goals. Albert Einstein famously stated that the definition of insanity is doing the same thing repeatedly while expecting different results. Thomas Edison is known for successfully discovering 8,000 ways not to make a light bulb. Abraham Lincoln didn't win an election until the presidential race. These exceptional American heroes undoubtedly utilized mistakes, setbacks, and failure as valuable feedback. How will you? The next time you experience a loss, ask yourself: What can I learn from this? How can I employ this experience to adjust my strategy or technique and move closer to my ultimate goal? Remember, behind every crisis lies a far more valuable opportunity.

Mistakes, Setbacks and Failure

"No one has ever achieved something great without encountering adversity. Mistakes are the portals to discovery."

—**James Joyce**, *Irish writer and poet*

A mistake, setback or loss is never the problem. The problem lies when we don't step back to learn from our mistakes. Mistakes provide feedback. The only mistake is not learning from it.

Next time you make a mistake, try not to judge it or yourself. Be aware of what happened and let it go. Trust yourself to make an adjustment the next time you're in the same situation.

List three mistakes you made in the last match you played:

1. _____

2. _____

3. _____

Choose one, and describe how you judged yourself at the time. _____

_____

_____

_____

_____

What do you notice when you talk to yourself this way? _____

_____

_____

_____

What could you say to yourself after a mistake that would be helpful? _____

_____

_____

_____

Create a mistake routine. What short routine could you do to help yourself let go of mistakes? Describe it. _____

_____

_____

_____

Workout 29
Mental Principles

- Winning isn't just about technique; it's about how you compete.

- Perfection is rarely required to win.

- Let go of expectations; they can't be controlled.

I'm Better—How Could I Lose!
The Seven Costliest Mistakes Made By the Favorite

Don't aim at success. The more you aim and make it a target, the more you are going to miss it. For success, like happiness, cannot be pursued; it must ensue… Happiness must happen, and the same holds for success: you have to let it happen by not caring about it. In the long run…success will follow you precisely because you had forgotten to think about it.

—**Victor Frankl**, *Man's Search for Meaning*

I'm Better—How Could I Lose!

Does this phrase sound familiar: 'I'm the better player, how did I lose?' Now, let's imagine this scenario: It was the first round of a local tournament, and you were playing against your recreational pickleball friends. The weather was hot and muggy, with the sun beaming down intensely. The time was 3 p.m., and many friends were watching. The match featured the heavily-favored team of Tom and Brian against their opponents, Steve and Rob. Although they had never met before, many people believed Tom and Brian were the stronger pair. Some even referred to Rob as a pushover, but he saw himself as a competitor.

The match didn't unfold as most had anticipated. Tom and Brian, who appeared confident during the warm-up, were taken aback by Rob's consistency and Steve's powerful shots. Somewhere along the way, Brian's morale took a hit. He started missing easy balls, chastising himself on a few occasions, and eventually found himself shaking hands at the net with his head hanging low. The final score stood at 11-9, 11-8. Tom and Brian were left stunned and bewildered. How could they lose to a team with strokes like that? However, one thing was clear to them—Rob and Steve never surrendered. They relentlessly chased down every seemingly unattainable ball and maintained a consistent level of play until the very last point.

All recreational, tournament, and even professional players have likely encountered this situation at least once in their competitive careers. However, how many of these players genuinely strive to understand what happened and create a plan to prevent the same thing from repeating itself in their next match?

This workout is designed to emphasize the biggest mistakes a favorite can make when facing a supposed underdog.

1. Overconfidence.

How many players have you witnessed starting a match with a sense of entitlement, believing that victory is guaranteed due to their seeding, technique, or past results? The pitfall of such a mindset is that it diverts a player's attention from the present moment and hinders their ability to perform at their best during the match by fixating on off-court factors.

2. Focus on winning

We all have a strong desire to win. However, it's crucial to remember that winning is not entirely within our control. We must acknowledge that our opponents also share the same desire to win. When a player finds themselves preoccupied with the end result, it is essential to redirect their focus towards the present moment and shift their attention to something they can control. They can ask themselves, "What do I need to do to play this point effectively?" It may begin with centering their focus on their breath and attaining a state of relaxation and centeredness. (Refer to Workout 11, "How to Play in the Moment: It's as Easy as Breathing.")

3. Listen to the hype

Your friends, teammates, and fans will shower you with praise. While it's pleasant to receive such accolades, they won't contribute a single point to your score. Your sole focus should be on how you can best prepare for the match. This mindset may not be glamorous, but if you heed the advice of true champions, you'll realize that this is how they approach every match. They direct their attention solely to what they can control and let go of the rest.

4. Relying on talent alone

Talent is undoubtedly valuable, as it can make learning a sport easier for some individuals compared to others. However, there comes a point where everyone encounters an opponent for whom talent alone is insufficient to secure victory. In fact, talent can sometimes become a curse for players who perceive their abilities as "sufficient" to achieve desired outcomes. Player development hinges on a combination of talent, work ethic, on-court intelligence, and the determination to compete. All these factors are essential in shaping a player's growth.

5. Lack of competitive intensity

If you were to inquire about the proportion of a match dedicated to competing versus playing at one's best, the answer would indicate that competing holds greater significance. It is exceedingly rare for someone to consistently perform at their absolute best. Nonetheless, a player can always exert control over their level of competitiveness.

6. Losing composure

It's true that as the favorite, there is an expectation for you to emerge victorious. Consequently, when the match becomes tight, the underdog gains inspiration, while you may start to feel frustrated. Before you realize it, negative self-talk takes hold, your paddle goes flying, and you lose control on the court. As the favorite, it is imperative to always be ready to give your utmost effort, maintain focus, and work diligently for every point, regardless of the skill level of your opponent.

7. Lack of awareness

Frequently, the favorite remains oblivious to the tactical and strategic dynamics unfolding on the court. This is often due to their preconceived notions of how the match should unfold. Once again, their focus veers towards the past or future, fixating on an ideal rather than embracing the present moment. It is crucial to approach the match without rigid expectations, except for the commitment to compete wholeheartedly and strive to deliver one's best performance. Cultivating an open mindset enables the player to perceive the unfolding events and make necessary adjustments accordingly.

I'm Better—How Could I Lose!

When athletes focus on what they cannot control, stress levels rise, breathing becomes rapid, muscles tense up, confidence diminishes, and performance suffers. This occurs because these factors are beyond their direct control and fluctuate from moment to moment.

When athletes focus on what they can control, they experience increased positivity, relaxation, and openness to opportunities. This is because the process is within their control.

Peak performance demands that athletes focus on what they can control.

List controllables and uncontrollables for your next match.

Controllables	Uncontrollables
Preparation	Weather (sun/wind/rain)

What does completing the table make you aware of? _____

_____

_____

_____

How can you use it to help you? _____

_____

_____

_____

"Without a struggle, there will be no progress.
- FREDERICK DOUGLASS

Workout 30
Mental Principles

- Little successes add up to big victories.
- Win or lose, you can always learn from your performance.
- The only loss occurs when you fail to learn.

Sweet Victory!
Seven Questions to Ask After a Win (or Loss)

ON COURT DRILL
Unforced Errors

Purpose: To illustrate to players precisely how they are winning or losing points, this drill aims to focus on the specific mechanics of point acquisition. In pickleball, the majority of games are determined by unforced errors. Therefore, this drill concentrates on the method of point acquisition rather than just the outcome.

Drill:
- Players can engage in either singles or doubles matches. The game follows these scoring rules:
- The initial game score is 0-0.
- The winner strives to reach +5 points.
- When a player commits an unforced error, they lose 1 point, while the opposing team's score remains unchanged.
- Players earn a point when they force their opponent into making an error.
- Points are also earned when a player hits a winner.

For instance, if two points are played and both teams make unforced errors, the score would be -1 to -1. If the first team subsequently hits a winner and forces an error, the score would become 1 to -1.

Progressions: This scoring system can be applied to dink games or any other game format. It enables players to analyze and determine whether they are winning through solid play or losing games due to errors.

Mental intention: The purpose is to comprehend the process of a point beyond the mere score. This approach empowers players to address the specific requirements of their game. Instead of getting frustrated with the result, they can concentrate on the strategies needed to win a point. The crucial aspect is to avoid negativity and establish a game plan that reduces unforced errors while putting pressure on the opponent.

Sweet Victory!

Many people often claim that you learn more from your losses than from your wins. Undoubtedly, there is some truth to this statement. Losses tend to leave a lasting impact and may highlight areas where things didn't go as planned. However, it would be a mistake to underestimate the valuable insights to be gained from both victories and defeats. It is crucial to remember that winning or losing is beyond your control. Consequently, a wise player looks beyond the outcomes and strives to improve regardless of the result.

Whether a player wins or loses, they should always ask themselves key questions about their performance. The objective of asking these questions is to heighten awareness of what transpired, enabling the analysis of both their own performance and that of their opponent. The rest of this workout will outline seven crucial questions that players should ask themselves following either a satisfying victory or a challenging loss.

1. Provide a brief description of the score and match conditions.

This question serves as an opportunity for the player to record the score and share their overall observations of the match. It could be as concise as, "I won 11-7, 4-11, 11-8. The courts were fast with no shade. I performed well in the first game,

experienced a decline in intensity during the second, but regained it in the third." The intention behind this question is not to pass judgment but rather to document the objective facts pertaining to the competition.

2. How did I feel mentally and physically before the competition?

It is crucial to check in with yourself and comprehend your state of mind and physical well-being to evaluate the areas that require attention. Often, a player might be riding the momentum of a significant victory, feeling mentally and physically fatigued from a long match, recovering from an injury, or returning to competition after a hiatus. All of these factors influence your preparation and performance, and thus should be acknowledged. By understanding these factors, a player becomes aware of the situation and can make necessary adjustments if needed. Furthermore, it allows the player to identify effective tactics that have yielded positive results and replicate them in future matches.

3. What are three things I did well?

It is essential to recognize our strengths and winning shot patterns during competition, as this enables us to continue utilizing and developing them. This awareness serves as feedback for further enhancement of our strengths. In any performance, there is seldom perfection, nor complete flawlessness. It typically lies somewhere in between. Undoubtedly, we all possess weaknesses, but our objective in competition is to position ourselves in a way that allows us to execute the shots we desire in the desired situations. By accomplishing this, we increase our chances of competing at our best and, consequently, winning. Possible responses to this question could be: "I executed strong returns and immediately transitioned from the transition zone to the kitchen" or "I displayed aggressive forward movement." Subsequently, ask yourself: How can I continue to build upon these positive aspects?

4. What are three areas in which I can improve?

Whether you have achieved a victory or experienced a loss, congratulations! If you have won, well done! If you have lost, hang in there! There are always opportunities for growth and refinement. Ask yourself: How can I incorporate these improvements into my next match?

5. If I played this opponent again, what would I do the same, and what would I do differently?

This question will help you analyze the strategic aspects of the competition. Ira Miller, a well-respected colleague, told me that "Winning is about making your opponent uncomfortable" with regard to shot selection.

6. What are my next steps, and who can assist me?

This is a crucial question that prompts the player to consider their future actions and identify individuals who can support their progress. The answer may involve short-term measures to prepare for the upcoming competition or long-term plans to advance to the next level in their development.

7. How do I feel about my effort and performance in the match?

Once again, this question serves as a self-check, allowing the player to assess their mental and physical state. An answer might be, "I'm exhausted, but I feel satisfied with my effort and I'm confident as I head into the finals tomorrow."

In summary, a player who takes the time to answer these questions after a match will gain heightened awareness of their mental, tactical, strategic, and physical aspects of the game. Moreover, documenting your matches and progress will provide valuable reference points for your continuous development, especially when facing the same player or someone with a similar playing style in future matches. Over time, players and coaches will discern trends and patterns that necessitate adjustments. Whether the outcome is a gratifying victory or a challenging loss, congratulations and remain resilient!

Sweet Victory!

Seven Questions to Ask After a Win (or Loss)

"The match doesn't end after the last point…that's actually the time to evaluate what happened, what you might do differently, and how you can improve next time."

—Rob Polishook

Date: _____

Tournament Match: _____   Recreational Game(s): _____

Doubles: _____   Singles: _____

Match location / weather: _____

Opponent's name(s) and team: _____

My partner's name: _____

Won: _____   Lost: _____   Score: _____

1. Describe the match: _____

_____

_____

_____

_____

_____

_____

2. **How did I feel mentally and physically coming into the match?** _____

_____

_____

3. **What are three things I did well?** _____

1. _____

2. _____

3. _____

4. **What are three things I didn't do well that I can improve on?** _____

1. _____

2. _____

3. _____

5. **If I played this opponent again, what would I do the same? What would I do differently?** _____

_____

_____

6. **What are my next steps to making these adjustments? Who can help me?** _____

_____

_____

7. **How did I feel about my effort and play regarding my match?** _____

_____

_____

_____

Workout 31
Mental Principles

- The athlete is a person first and a performer second.
- Choking happens!
- Our biggest fears usually surface when we feel most vulnerable.

Fight, Flight, Freeze
The Seven Biggest Fears that Paralyze Athletes

ON COURT DRILL
Third Shot Drop/Drive

Purpose: Arguably, the third shot drop is the most crucial shot in the game. It facilitates a player or team in transitioning from defense to neutral or from neutral to offense. Given its significance, we must devise a method to replicate the pressure and the execution of this shot.

Drill:
- The serving player serves 10 times, alternating sides to the returning player.
- After serving, the returning player returns the ball and advances to the net.
- The serving player must then execute a third shot drop.
- Successfully executing the third shot drop earns the serving player a point.
- If the third shot drop is unsuccessful, the serving player does not earn a point.

Progressions:
- The server can choose to mix in drives instead of drops
- Alternatively, players can choose to play the point to completion after the serve. Then they have two scores. The first is how many successful drops or drives were executed, and whether they won the point.
- Regardless of the variation chosen, the game concludes after 10 points.
- The serving player then assesses how many points they won out of the ten tries and how many third shots or drives were made.

Mental Intention: Obviously, the goal is to score after a serve; however, the returning side has an advantage as they can reach the kitchen first. This drill informs the server about the percentage of points they can score on their serve and, how effective third shot drops, drives, or a combination of both are. Each player or team should practice this drill multiple times during each practice session, aiming to raise their percentage of points won off the serve.

Fight, Flight, Freeze

How many times have you thought the following: "If only I could play to my potential…" "If only I could play matches like I practice…" "If only I wouldn't get tight during crucial points…" "If only I could just play…" "I'm so much better than this, but…" and so on and so forth? We all know the immense importance of the mental side of tennis. Dr. Alan Goldberg, a renowned mental training coach, affirms, "In sports, the mental game is like glue—it's what holds everything together."

Pickleball is made up of four parts: technical, strategic, physical, and mental. One of these parts without the others is essentially worthless. You can think of it like a car. The technical part is the body—a stable foundation, streamlined to make the car travel smoothly. The strategic part is the steering wheel—able to travel in the desired direction or change course whenever necessary. The physical part is the gas—physical preparation and stamina, the component ensuring that the car has the juice to complete the journey. The mental part is the engine—the most essential component, the force that starts the car and makes it run. When all of the above are working smoothly together, our pickleball game runs like a brand new sports car, with high performance and no worries. Yet when one of the components goes awry, the whole car malfunctions.

Knowing all this, the key question becomes: What hinders a player from performing well in pressure situations? More often than not, it results from fears that obstruct the path toward unlimited potential performance. Often, the player is aware of these fears but does not accept them, leading to internal conflict. At other times, the fears may lie just beneath their conscious thought patterns, requiring a deeper exploration of what truly underlies those fears. Following are seven significant fears that can impede an athlete from reaching their unlimited performance potential.

1. Fear of Not Being Good Enough.

This fear surfaces frequently, both on and off the court. In fact, merely contemplating it can trigger an "aha" moment. We all aspire to believe in ourselves and possess the capacity for success, so falling short of that can be disheartening. During match play, players may become discouraged and start fearing that they are inadequate to compete against an opponent, leading to a loss of will and less-than-optimal performance. In life, and in pickleball, setbacks can sometimes feel like confirmation of our perceived inadequacy, as if we lacked what it takes to succeed. However, while setbacks may occur, our true strength lies in how we respond to them.

2. Fear of Failure.

This fear typically emerges during a close match, particularly when a player or team is deemed superior to their opponent. The player who is seen as less skilled often competes without expectations, while the favored player appears burdened by the weight of expectations. The favored player is afraid to fail because they link their identity and self-worth to their performance. Furthermore, they may fear judgment from others if they fall short of expectations. Often, when a player is hesitant to experiment, reluctant to try new techniques, or unwilling to take risks, their fear of failure is the underlying factor.

3. Fear of the Unknown.

This fear often manifests itself during the preparation for a significant match. The player cannot definitively know whether they will emerge victorious or experience defeat. This "fear of the unknown" generates heightened anxiety about what might unfold, leading to concerns about subsequent events and outcomes. Accompanying this fear is the apprehension of losing control. This is evident when a player finds themselves in a defensive stance. In such instances, the player may over-hit, try to speed up prematurely, attempt risky shots in the hopes of achieving an improbable winner, simply because they feel uncomfortable with their opponent dictating the flow of the point. However, recognizing their defensive positioning and accepting the situation will enable them to play solid defense, gradually regaining control and working their way back to a neutral position.

4. Fear of Being Judged.

This fear frequently arises when a player contemplates what others might think of their performance during the game. This shift in focus draws the player away from their present situation on the court, diverting their attention towards external factors beyond their control. At this point, the significance of receiving unconditional acceptance from the support team becomes paramount. When such support is provided, the player can experience a sense of calm, relaxation, and security. As a result, they can play with a liberated mindset, devoid of any concerns about the outcomes.

5. Fear of Not Meeting Expectations.

This fear shares similarities with the fear of being judged, as both involve the player's inability to control the expectations others have of them. Frequently, the expectations placed on the player by friends, teammates, and others revolve solely around wins and losses, disregarding the significance of the process and the journey itself. To unlock their best performance, a player must remain present and fully immersed in the experience. Shifting their focus towards expectations of winning can serve as a mental distraction and hinder their performance.

6. Fear of Success.

This fear becomes evident when a player gains a lead and starts entertaining thoughts such as, "I shouldn't be defeating this person—they have a higher ranking than me." Alternatively, the player may perceive themselves as lacking a certain skill level and consequently feel undeserving of a victory. In other instances, the uncertainty and resulting anxiety of exposing oneself to the possibility of success become overwhelming. The certainty of losing, albeit disappointing, is a familiar path already traveled.

7. Fear of Injury or Re-Injury.

This fear is often referred to as the "silent epidemic" by sport psychologist Dr. David Grand. It stems from our sports culture's reluctance to address the emotional stress and traumatic experiences that can result from injuries. Specifically, it overlooks the athlete's uncertainties about recovery, feelings of detachment from the team, fear of not regaining full strength, and even anxiety about the possibility of a recurrence. It's important to note that while the athlete may receive physical clearance from doctors, they may still grapple with emotional unease and unresolved fears. Those who have experienced an injury understand that the mental scars do not simply vanish when the doctor declares them fit to play.

In today's sporting society, displaying any indication of weakness or fear can be challenging for a player. Society tends to perceive vulnerability as a sign of weakness, but in truth, acknowledging our vulnerability is a testament to genuine strength. Fears, including the seven mentioned earlier, frequently arise, particularly in high-pressure situations. They serve as defense mechanisms, preventing us from engaging in activities that might make us uncomfortable. However, recognizing these fears and possessing the courage and support system to navigate through them is what genuinely empowers us to evolve and unlock our individual potential.

Fight, Flight, Freeze

The Seven Biggest Fears That Paralyze Athletes

Rate these fears in order of how they affect you:

	Fear of not being good enough		Fear of not meeting expectations
	Fear of failure		Fear of success
	Fear of the unknown		Fear of injury/re-injury
	Fear of being judged		Other (did I miss one?)

Choose the top fear and write it here: _____

When you think of this fear, what do you experience? _____

_____

What is the scariest aspect about that fear? _____

On a scale of 1 to 10 (10 being the most), how strong is the fear? _____

How do you feel the experience on the court (i.e. tight/restricting)? _____

_____

Where do you feel the fear in your body? _____

Now, bring your attention to a time on the court when you felt calm. How did you experience it? _____

_____

Where do you feel the calm in your body? _____

Now, take a minute to notice the calm. Go back to noticing the fear . . . how do you experience it now? _____

_____

Usually the fear will subside.

Workout 32
Mental Principles

- An athlete is a person first and performer second.

- When an athlete walks onto the court, their experiences, fears, day-to-day issues follow them.

- Everyone gets nervous and can choke, what's important is how they bounce back.

I Can't Believe I Choked!
Understanding Slumps, Blocks and the Yips

Mental Practices from Ben Johns ...

@benjohns.pb

Find your calm mental state

Be present in the moment

Create a reset reminder

Focus on accomplishment more than obstacles

Move on from last point

Work on making this (mental game) a habit

I Can't Believe I Choked!

How many times have you seen a pickleball player get tight, under-perform, or choke in a big event? In practice, they play great—not a care in the world, going for broke on every shot, and effortlessly succeeding while doing so. Yet once the competition starts, their best shots become their worst. Perhaps their big serve, previously a weapon, goes long. Or maybe the formerly simple act of a third-shot drop now becomes unmanageable. Suddenly, the reliable returner can't make a routine return. Inexplicably, the player in the kitchen hesitates during a pivotal point and misses the speed-up. Fans become dumbfounded and cannot believe that this great player is affected by this type of pressure. "How can this happen? What's the cause of this?" they ask.

In looking for the solution, many coaches, fans, players, media, and even performance experts start by critiquing what they can see (i.e., the missed third shot, missed return, or errant serve). Their initial intent is to look above the surface to find what's broken in hopes of a technical "quick fix." Certainly, this is the place to look if the situation occurs once or twice. However, if the choke or slump continues repeatedly under pressure, it falls into the category of a repetitive sports performance block.

A repetitive sports performance block (i.e., choke, slump, yips) is actually the symptom of an underlying issue. The cause is an accumulation of negative experiences from which the athlete has not been able to move on. In actuality, this block has little to do with the last time the player "choked." Rather, something about that pressure situation was the trigger that brought the unprocessed issue to the surface, distracting the pickleball player's performance. In fact, before or during the competition, some athletes are aware that "something is just not right." They experience underlying nervousness and anxiety and try to hide or resist it. Oftentimes, the player doesn't want to address their anxiety for fear of being judged by teammates or others as lacking mental toughness. Yet other times, the player may be completely unaware of the root cause of their anxiety since it has been dissociated from their consciousness in an effort to protect their personal psyche. Either way, the athlete's performance bears the burden.

Much like "heavy baggage" we hold onto on a daily basis, these negative experiences can grip a person and accumulate during their life from both on-and off-field incidents. Emotional trauma can come from situations such as embarrassment from missing serves in a big match, missing an overhead, or repeatedly missing dinks on your soft game. Physical trauma can stem from getting hit with a ball, falling on a court, or even tripping on a wide forehand. Additionally, off-field trauma can occur and accumulate, resulting from issues such as relationship problems, death, car accidents, or other circumstances. Similarly, excessive judgment, expectations, and comparisons to opponents from parents, coaches, media, or friends can unknowingly add weight to the burden of pressure and distract a player from playing freely.

Throughout our lives, we encounter physical and emotional trauma. Depending on the severity of these instances and our preparedness to meet them at the time, we sometimes successfully absorb and process these encounters, while other times we do not. When we are unable to process these experiences, the stress does not evaporate over time. Instead, we store the unprocessed memory in the brain, where it may manifest itself at unexpected times. For example, during a game, a pickleball player may be so scared of losing or making the same error from previous matches that they tense up, hesitate, or even freeze during the match.

These unprocessed negative experiences can accumulate like balls in a bucket. Each individual issue represents a different-sized ball. Some may be as small as a golf ball, while others are larger, like a tennis ball or even a pickleball, depending on the level of stress and anxiety the person/athlete carries. These emotional and physical trauma-like experiences get held in the body's central nervous system, directly interfering with the player's ability to access and adapt to situations and perform movements that were once so easy and instinctual. Finally, when a ball tumbles out of the bucket, the player's repetitive sports performance block is now on public display for all to see, judge, and evaluate.

We often forget that behind the superstar athlete's exterior, the athlete is a person first and a performer second. It's almost impossible not to be affected by the troubling day-to-day events that we all experience. Each person holds on to different things in different ways. James Blake summed it up best in his autobiography, Breaking Back, when he explained, "If there is something wrong in your life, it will show up in your tennis game—not always in predictable ways…self-belief might be manifested in weak second serves, impatience can cause you to make low-percentage gambles, and so on."

In summary, it's clear that we hold emotional fears and physical injuries in our bodies, akin to trauma-like experiences. As individuals, this "baggage" can consciously or unconsciously affect how we react, adapt, and adjust to everyday situations. As athletes, it can also carry onto the playing field and impact their performance, particularly in high-pressure situations. Given this, it makes sense to look beyond the slump, choke, or yips and delve into the root cause. The athlete is not broken or a "head case," as some might suggest. The block is part of their process and can actually provide valuable clues to turning their situation around. Ultimately, they will emerge mentally stronger, move without hesitation, and compete with increased confidence.

I Can't Believe I Choked!

Think of a time you choked or got really uptight...when was it? Where was it? Who were you playing?

_____

_____

_____

What did you try to do at the time to try and manage the situation?

_____

_____

_____

Describe in detail what happened, and what you experienced...

Before: _____

_____

_____

During: _____

_____

_____

After: _____

_____

_____

Has it happened in another area of your life, on or off the court? Describe it.

_____

_____

_____

_____

_____

Recognizing the above, what does this make you aware of?

_____

_____

_____

What are three things you could try next time as you feel yourself starting to get tense?

1. _____

2. _____

3. _____

PLAY B.A.D.

Bᴀsɪᴄs Aʟʟ Dᴀʏ

Conclusion

What's Next?

Pickleball Inside the Zone is intended to stimulate ideas, thoughts, and questions. Ultimately, the workbook is designed to provide a foundation to help you become more self-aware, curious, and embrace competition throughout your athletic journey. Just like any journey, different events and experiences will bring different insights. Be aware of these insights and continually build upon them.

Pickleball Inside the Zone is meant to continually evolve and guide you back to a centered place, regardless of where you are on your competitive journey. Therefore, I encourage you to revisit and reassess the workouts throughout your journey. From my experience, any path to improvement is taken one step at a time. This process requires patience, purpose, and perseverance, both for others and for yourself. It reminds me of the Chinese proverb, 'A journey of a thousand miles begins with a single step.'

Now that you have read and experienced *Pickleball Inside the Zone*, I thank you for your time and hope you have found it both rewarding and thought provoking. I invite you to share your insights, experiences, successes, failures, and obstacles with me. I genuinely look forward to reconnecting with you in my future books, workshops, or consultations.

My Next Step...

As I mentioned, just like your personal journey, mine is also evolving. In the Introduction, I mentioned how this book began with my clients asking me questions about mental training. Little did I know at the time that it would eventually lead to the publication of my fourth book!

But as we know, no journey is complete without taking the next step... My next step is to select certain key chapters and expand on them in another book. With this in mind, I have already started writing a book called *The Whole Human Athlete: The Journey Beyond the Score*. Following that, I will be working on *Doggedness: Mental Skills Athletes Can Learn from Animals*. Stay tuned for more exciting additions and developments in the future, as we continue to expand upon the valuable content and insights shared in this book.

B'simcha (with happiness)

Rob

P.S. If you want to chat more, share an idea, experience, or thought, agree or disagree with something I said, please contact me at:

rob@insidethezone.com
www.insidethezone.com
973-723-0314

I'll look forward to hearing from you!

Biography of the Author

Rob Polishook, M.A., C.P.C., is the founder and director of Inside the Zone Sports Performance Group, LLC. As a mental training coach, he works with athletes and teams from junior players to professionals, helping them to uncover their mental edge—often the difference between winning and losing. He specializes in helping athletes overcome performance blocks (i.e. yips, chokes, slumps, anxiety), helping athletes work through the "unspoken" psychological trauma from injuries, helping already high-performing athletes reach beyond self-imposed barriers, and teaching innovative mental training skills, tools, and techniques.

Rob's non-judgmental manner encourages athletes to work with performance issues using awareness, acceptance, and brain/body intuition. This unique inside out approach encourages empowerment and trust in self and the process. Rob's focus is on the athlete as a person first and a performer second which he coined Whole Human Athlete. Through this lens he recognizes that day-to-day, on and off-the-court experiences directly impact how an athlete performs especially under pressure.

Rob has presented workshops in India, Israel and the United States. He regularly runs week-long workshops called "Unleashing the Performer Within" at the highly acclaimed Omega Institute. Additionally, his articles have been published nationally and internationally and he has been quoted in *Sports Illustrated*. He has also been featured in interviews with ESPN radio.

Rob has earned a Masters degree in psychological studies with a concentration in sport and exercise psychology from Seton Hall University (SHU) and has completed his certification in sport psychology from SHU. He is a certified professional/life coach from IPEC, an international federation coaching affiliate. He has also received certifications in Somatic Experiencing, Brainspotting Sports Performance Work, Focusing and Jim Loehr's Mental Toughness Program. Additionally, he is a certified Mindfulness teacher and incorporates spirituality and animal wisdom into his teachings.

Rob and his wife Debbie live in New York City. He can often be spotted walking his dog Gumbo in Central park and/or having coffee with his wife Debbie at a neighborhood coffee shop.

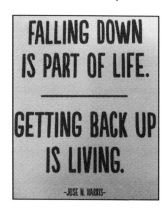

FALLING DOWN IS PART OF LIFE.

GETTING BACK UP IS LIVING.

-JOSE N. HARRIS-

About *Inside the Zone* **Performance Group**

Founded in 2005, Inside the Zone Sports Performance Group was born from Rob Polishook's passion for sports, his love of working with kids, and his curiosity in understanding the process of what it takes to help athletes break beyond obstacles, challenges and barriers. The goal of Inside the Zone Sports Performance Group is to assist athletes and pickleball players, at all levels, to uncover their mental edge and unleash their unlimited peak performance.

The mental side plays a large role in all sports. It is remiss that the real mental issues regarding competition, focus, goals, nerves, and the athlete as a person first are not being addressed. These issues include but are not limited to:

- Competing under pressure
- Dealing with adversity and using them to bounce back
- Handling pressure and expectations
- Concentrating under pressure
- Staying centered, balanced and calm
- Focusing on the process and not on the outcome
- Crafting strategies for goal setting
- Reaching beyond self imposed barriers

Inside the Zone Sports Performance Group offers the following services:

- One-on-one and group consultations for athletes, parents, and coaches
- Workshops and seminars for teams, parents, and coaches
- Dynamic season-long consultations for teams

Rob Polishook, M.A., C.P.C.
Mental Training Coach

www.insidethezone.com
@insidethezone.com
rob@insidethezone.com

Whole Human Athlete™
Heart . Energy . Spirit

About Rob: *The Back Story*

Who am I?

I was born imperfect—or maybe perfectly imperfect! Here's a great example from my first-grade class trip: All I remember is spinning around a revolving door at the Empire State Building, getting my shoe caught, and holding everyone up from accessing the door for three minutes while being laughed at by my classmates. Once we were back in the classroom, I struggled to read. The letters were a jumbled mess, teachers would get frustrated, and I felt ashamed to raise my hand. I was diagnosed with a form of dyslexia and a motor learning problem.

I vividly remember being left behind in first grade and attempting to explain the reason to my friends. Even clearer was my memory of receiving special tutoring from Mrs. Schaffer after school for reading, writing, and arithmetic. By the time I reached third grade, I still couldn't read or write in cursive, which posed a problem. It felt like being in a foreign country. The only place where I might have felt normal was Hebrew school, but there I struggled with understanding the Hebrew letters and the fact that they were read from right to left. During my spare time, I recall balancing on a board, the kind with a roller underneath, which was supposed to help with my coordination and balance.

I did these types of exercises throughout my entire childhood! Extra work was ingrained in my upbringing. I never had time to feel sorry for myself or ask why I was different; I simply attended extra tutoring and spent hours on my balance board.

I learned at an early age to never, never, never give up. I never let an opportunity for extra credit pass me by, and I never stopped training in anything I cared about.

I was fortunate. At an early age, I experienced the presence of a strong support system with parents who believed in me. Due to my learning disabilities, I developed empathy towards others who didn't accomplish tasks as quickly or as effectively as the rest of the class.

Why am I writing this book?

Every day, I listen to athletes in various sports, including pickleball, sharing their fears, anxieties, and performance issues with me. I hear how they stand at the baseline feeling like they are on a deserted island, or how they constantly get caught in a negative thought spiral during pressure situations or before a big game. It reminds me of my own childhood, where I wished I had someone to whom I could open up and express how I was feeling, someone who would understand my perspective. Instead, my coaches always dictated how I should feel and what I could or couldn't do. If nothing else, a book like this would have been invaluable for providing an outlet to let go and, in some cases, to validate that my thoughts were "normal".

After listening to what my clients are saying, I usually reassure them that they are not alone in their thoughts and feelings. In fact, their thoughts and feelings are often shared by many athletes in similar situations at all levels. This reassurance often makes them feel like a 500-pound weight has been lifted off their shoulders. When I tell them that they are not broken and don't need fixing, that the answers lie within themselves, and that we just need to uncover them, they usually take a deep breath and exhale in relief.

Rob, Deb, and Gumbo

Acknowledgments

A book like this doesn't happen without the support and encouragement of many people.

First, and foremost I'd like to thank my dear friend Krishna Yerrmosu. We have played together, drilled together, and competed against each other many times on the court. However, our real connection was forged during our walks en route to the courts. During these walks, we discussed our intentions for that day. One day, it may have been to be more aware of "out balls"and to let them go. On another day, our intentions might have centered around driving the ball less forcefully and incorporating more third-shot drops and resets from the transition area. Then, on our walks home, we would discuss how we adhered to our intentions, share thoughts on our games and each other's games. It was clear to me that Krishna is not only passionate about the game but has a keen eye for the mental aspect and an understanding of its importance. He has been a sounding board and has also shared many of his ideas which have been instrumental in the organizational, development and editing process. This book wouldn't have come to fruition without Krishna's friendship, energy, focus and attention to detail.

Next up are Justin Dadges, Alex Kidder, Regina Zafonte, Sam Priven, Patrick Schmidt, Alex Miller, Steve Peretz, Jonathan Kutzin, Tom Pryor, Tom Schnepp, Ricardo Baldwin, and Deb Polishook. They are all great drilling partners and friends who have generously shared their knowledge, drills, and insights.

Special thanks to Papo, Eddie, Gary, Listra, Joe, Huddy, Carlos, Dominick, Adam, Andrew, Victoria, Vera and everyone else at Central Park who welcomed me into the game and have shared their passions. Thanks also to Joe, Lion, Chase, Shay, Jay and others at Miami Beach Pickleball Club Courts. And lastly, thanks to John, Rick, Bob, Steve, Eric, Guy, Sandy, and my friends at the mid-coast Pegasus courts in Brunswick, Maine

Major thanks to John Reinhardt, who single-handedly formatted and assisted with many design decisions. Big thanks always to Kellie Patterson, as she has been instrumental in all the graphic development and the *Inside the Zone* creative process.

A big hug and thanks to my wife, Debbie. None of this work could have ever begun without your unconditional love, support, and belief in me. Finally, thanks to Gumbo, as she patiently sits in my office while I work.

Made in the USA
Las Vegas, NV
19 November 2024

12106037R00122